For my wife, Kelly.

You always stand with me, beside me, in front of me, and behind me as I plow through every day, passionately living life to the fullest.

"I really like this book! I like how Jan paints a candid portrait of what life can be like when we deal with abusive relationships, addictions, hopelessness, and various other curve balls life is guaranteed to throw our way. But even more than that, I like the way Jan masterfully paints a portrait of hope, pointing us to the promises of the Scriptures, while using practical, heartfelt stories—like his troubled friend from Indiana—to remind us that God has created a way out of our painful or tragic story.

Exodus of Our Lives takes us on an inspiring journey from self-centered living to what Jan calls the "Altruistic Journey." To emphasize the focus of this journey, Jan points us to Helen Keller's poignant words, "Better to be blind and see with your heart, than to have two good eyes and see nothing."

So, if you're asking questions like: Why is this happening to me? What's the purpose of my life? Even if you're simply challenging the religious status quo in search of a deeper, more meaningful relationship with Jesus, then this book is for you! I recommend that you invite your friends and family to take the journey with you in reading *Exodus of Our Lives*."

—*Pastor Joseph Thompson, Executive Director of Spiritual Development, Action Church, Winter Springs, FL*

"Prepare to embark on an adventure where you are sure to be challenged, encouraged, stirred, and changed. Using the Exodus story as a roadmap, Jan interweaves his personal journey, Biblical teaching, and life principles to provide a helpful guide to finding faith, freedom, and fulfillment in the exhilarating journey with Jesus. Jan's transparency and humor are both refreshing and impacting. Wherever you are in your journey, you will glean valuable insight in getting unstuck from the fear, failure, and status quo that is keeping you from moving forward. I commend Jan's work to you, it will serve you well."

—*Dan Mastrapa, Lead Pastor, Sent Church*

"I've never liked driving to new places. I have the worst sense of direction. Even the thought of getting lost causes a sense of panic. Some time ago I started out on a new journey in life, a faith journey. I had that same sense of panic, as if I might get lost on the journey, which at times seemed unfamiliar and terrifying.

As I read *Exodus of Our Lives* I began to understand that I wouldn't find these journeys in my life so frightening if I just prepared for them.

I began to look inward asking myself, "Am I really applying God's word to my life or am I just reading and hearing his word on a surface level?"

As I read these pages, I began to discover the heart of Jesus. As I dug deeper into *Exodus of Our Lives* I realized I could do better if I began applying the wisdom Jesus shared through the Beatitudes to my own life.

I began to truly mourn the sin in my life and made the decision to be baptized. I was struggling with issues at work and started to see I often reacted poorly. Before this, I never even recognized when my reactions made things worse. As I continued reading *Exodus of Our Lives*, I read; "Blessed are the peacemakers, for they shall be called sons of God." I applied this Beatitude to my situations and, what do you know, things started getting better at work!

I also asked myself, "Am I striving to do the right thing when handling situations and making decisions in my life? I really didn't like the answer I found deep inside of myself! I realized I had been making many decisions and seeking answers that I thought benefitted me.

I read and reread, "Blessed are those who hunger and thirst for righteousness, for they shall be satisfied." Now, when the need to make a decision or deal with a situation arises, I immediately ask myself, "What is the right thing to do in God's eyes?" I often find the right thing to do is not the easy thing to do, but it is the best thing to do. The results are always worth the effort.

Exodus of Our Lives is now an invaluable tool in helping to navigate the journeys in my life and I know it will be for you as well. I am finding my promised land. You can too!"

—*Melissa "Izzy" Lamprey, Early Childhood Educator*

EXODUS OF OUR LIVES

Finding Your Promised Land

JAN PUTERBAUGH

SPIRITUAL ✝ THERAPY PUBLISHING

Exodus of Our Lives: Finding Your Promised Land by Jan Puterbaugh
Copyright © 2018

SPIRITUAL THERAPY PUBLISHING

Spiritual Therapy Publishing
120 Borada Rd
Sanford, FL 32773

SpiritualTherapyPub.com

First Printing: September 2018

ISBN: 978-1-7324037-2-7 (Paperback), 978-1-7324037-1-0 (Kindle), 978-1-7324037-0-3 (epub)

Cover Design: DesignByStacy.com
Copy and Content Editing: StaceyCovell.com
Publishing and Design Services: MartinPublishingServices.com

Scriptures taken from the Holy Bible, New International Version®, NIV®.
Copyright © 1973, 1978, 1984, 2011 by Biblica, Inc.™
Used by permission of Zondervan. All rights reserved worldwide. www.zondervan.com.
The "NIV" and "New International Version" are trademarks registered in the
United States Patent and Trademark Office by Biblica, Inc.™

ACKNOWLEDGEMENTS

Writing this book would not have been possible without these wonderful and amazing people:

TO MY BETA-READERS: Melissa "Izzy" Lamprey and Jeff DiMario. Your thoughtful input and the many hours spent reading the early manuscript helped me insure thoughts were stated clearly and easily understood. The friendship and the many conversations we share are a great source of encouragement.

TO MY KICKSTARTER BACKERS: Your faith and financial support was a great source of encouragement and made publishing this book possible. Thank you to all who pre-ordered and a special thanks to Pastor Phil Ayres & Stefanie, Jeff & Ileana DiMario, Mark & Carole Caraker, Jennifer Gerth, Mehdi Daryadel & Alison Puterbaugh, Greg & Laura Martin, Chuck & Dabney Klein and Melissa "Izzy" Lamprey.

TO MY PUBLISHING TEAM: Thank you to my editor, Stacey Covell, for working with me word by word and thought by thought. Your professional and creative input greatly enhanced this book. Thank you to Stacy Edwards for a beautiful cover and graphic design; to Melinda Martin for professional and careful interior design and marketing expertise; and to Pastor Phil Ayres for his ongoing encouragement, mentoring, and for writing the foreword. Thank you to my proofreaders, Kelly Puterbaugh and Melissa "Izzy" Lamprey. Your last pass proofreading ferreted out all the small extra words and misspellings that survived the vigorous editing process. You put the icing on this cake!

TO MY WONDERFUL FAMILY: A very special thank you to my wife, Kelly; my daughters and son's-in-law, Jessica & Mike and Shannon & Tim; and my five grandsons, Liam, Aiden, Isaac, Rhys and Kieran. Our daily interactions bring great joy and meaning to my life. I could not have done this without you.

AND FINALLY, TO MY AMAZING CHURCH FAMILY: LifePoint Christian Church, you are a never ending well of encouragement, your faith amazes me and your willingness to serve others inspires me. Keep loving Jesus, keep loving the least of these, keep being his hands and feet and most of all — keep being the church.

CONTENTS

FOREWORD / 1

INTRODUCTION / 3

CHAPTER 1
Contemplating the Journey / 5

CHAPTER 2
Getting Ready To Go / 15

CHAPTER 3
Attitudes That Build Our Hearts: The Blessed Attitudes / 23

CHAPTER 4
Attitudes That Guide Our Hearts: The Strength within You / 35

CHAPTER 5
Develop Your Plan / 45

CHAPTER 6
The Hardest Part is Leaving / 61

CHAPTER 7
Focusing on the Journey / 73

CHAPTER 8
The Promised Land / 89

APPENDIX 1
Applying the Beatitudes / 101

APPENDIX 2
Praying Without Ceasing / 104

APPENDIX 3
Recognizing the Opposing Forces / 106

APPENDIX 4
The Armor of God: Tools You Need on Your Journey / 110

APPENDIX 5
A Note Concerning Miracles / 114

APPENDIX 6
Hearing God's Voice / 117

BOOK COVER IMAGERY MEANING / 121

ABOUT THE AUTHOR / 123

Foreword

PHIL AYRES

The first time I met Jan Puterbaugh, I was the brand-new worship leader at a church that was not even one year old. It was an early Sunday morning prior to service and Jan was carrying a stack of folding chairs across a school cafeteria. When someone introduced me to him he dropped the chairs momentarily, thrust his hand out and said, "Hey, welcome to the family!"

That was 15 years ago, and you can still almost always find him moving some chairs around on a Sunday morning before church. He doesn't do this because that is all he's qualified to do; he moves those chairs because he has a pure servant's heart and there is nothing he won't do if it serves God's kingdom.

When Jan asked me to write the foreword for his book my mind flashed back to the thousands of hours we have spent working together for our church family, LifePoint. In the last decade and a half, we've set up literally hundreds of thousands of chairs. We have carried and pieced together thousands of stage pieces. We've assembled a ton of lighting arrangements and sound systems, projectors, and screens, plus countless tables for indoor and outdoor events. To date, our church family has gathered more than 800 times since 2002 and, by my count, Jan has only missed one service during that time because he was sick.

Jan is relentlessly positive. This sometimes bugs me; not because he shouldn't be optimistic all the time, but because I wish I could be the same way. In all the time I have known Jan I have rarely seen him angry or cross with another person. He and I have only ever had one argument—which is saying a lot considering we have worked together for so long (the disagreement was quickly resolved, apologies back and forth, etc.).

I say all this not because I'm trying to convince you that Jan is a good person. No, I say it because even though Jan is all these things, he has not had a perfect life. This is exactly why he was uniquely suited to write *Exodus of Our Lives*. Early on in our friendship Jan shared many of his past challenges with me, challenges that he will also share with you in the following pages.

He is qualified to write a book about personal exodus journeys because he has lived it.

What you're about to read is a real story of a man who has followed God despite the challenges of addiction and personal loss. I'm confident that as you read his story you'll see parallels in your own life. That's because *Exodus of Our Lives* is everyone's story, starting with the Israelites in Egypt and ending with you. Through the pages, you'll notice Pastor Jan's intention is far more than storytelling. He's also written this book to serve as your roadmap out of bondage.

If you're struggling with addiction, personal loss, or any other circumstance that holds you back from pure spiritual freedom, this book is the encouragement you need. *Exodus of Our Lives* will help you navigate your way forward, out of the darkness and into the light.

I'm confident that you'll enjoy and appreciate this book for its honesty, humor, and truth. May God bless you on your journey to the promised land.

> Phil Ayres
> Lead Pastor
> LifePoint Christian Church
> Author of *Flannel-Graph Jesus:*
> *More Than A One-Dimensional Savior*

Introduction

There are times in our lives when we recognize we need to regroup to move ahead, when we need to embark on a journey. Maybe we find ourselves in bondage on some level; maybe we feel called to step out of our familiar existence and move into uncharted waters. Or maybe we are simply moving into a new phase of life.

The question is this: How do we prepare for the journey so we can make it to the destination?

A few years ago, as my wife and I embarked on a journey through Atlanta, Georgia on our way to a mountain cabin deep in the Chattahoochee National Forest, memories from my youth started flooding back to my mind. You see, I was fifty-seven years old, well adjusted (whatever that means), happily married, and living the life of my dreams as an associate pastor in a small church in Longwood, Florida. I thought about the many journeys it had taken in getting to this place in life.

The traffic was heavy that day as it flowed through downtown Atlanta like a stream snaking down the mountains carrying everything caught in its current. I was taken aback as I remembered my life in the 1980's. I was in my twenties then and felt like I could tame the world. I have always had an unwavering passion for life, for experiences, and the unique beauty of my surroundings, whatever and wherever that might be.

I never doubted I could "make it" in life. The world was mine to conquer. Though my ambitions were tempered by the reality of daily living, I woke up each day with a drive to plow through life on my own, like an explorer headed out into the wilderness hoping to discover a vast paradise.

I was passionately in love with my high school sweetheart and had moved to Georgia and joined the Army just so I could be near her. While this might sound romantic and adventurous, I was also becoming a drug addict and making terrible decisions. I was an impulsive, passionate, drug addicted young person without a clue. It was a dangerous combination.

So here I was in Atlanta once again. More old memories and ghosts of their experiences flooded my mind: hiking up Stone Mountain and camping on the steep side (even though we weren't supposed to camp there), looking at the vast expanse of God's creation from Kennesaw Mountain and feeling the presence of soldiers who skirmished in the fields below, walking through

Underground Atlanta—an entertainment district under the viaducts deep in the city—and experiencing people from all walks of life; all of these overwhelmed me. I had thought all these adventures were the answer to fulfillment in life. In reality, I was navigating on my own aimlessly.

When I was young I was taught to be my own man, to be independent, that anything I achieved would be done by my own willpower. My parents didn't necessarily teach me this, society did. The message is everywhere. From Burger King's motto, "Have it Your Way," to every store trying to personalize your experience so you will buy more, we often grow up feeling like we are the center of existence. Even spiritually, we often feel we are the center of God's world. In fact, some preachers want you to think that. Why? Just like the stores, it's savvy marketing. When everything is centered on you, the more likely you are to keep coming back for more in that elusive quest to reach the top of the mountain.

As I have looked at my own journey and the journeys of so many others, I have seen so much in common with the Exodus story in Scripture where Moses led God's people out of bondage through the wilderness to the promised land.

Jesus wants us to view life as a journey and to embrace each season on this journey. Jesus wants us to be free from the bondage of ourselves. He wants us to find true fulfillment in life—fulfillment that can only be found in Him. When we make our lives all about God, all about Jesus and others around us, we find true fulfillment and freedom. This, my friend, is the promised land!

There are often several legs on the journey that make up the pieces of our larger quest to reach the promised land. This book will help you identify the journey you may be on or about to embark on, prepare using Biblical principles, and lay the groundwork to help you navigate the many obstacles and pitfalls which often keep us from reaching the sacred place God has for us. Additionally, I want you to know the secret of living in the promised land once you arrive.

As you read these pages, as you possibly see yourself in this narrative so many of us share, my prayer is you will be given the strength to depart on this journey and the knowledge of what to expect along the way, so you will be able to enter and live in your promised land.

Let's prepare for the Exodus of our lives.

1
Contemplating the Journey

The only impossible journey is the one you never begin.
—Tony Robbins

Then they said to him,
"Please inquire of God to learn
whether our journey will be successful."

The priest answered them,
"Go in peace. Your journey has the LORD's approval."

—Judges 18:5-6

We often identify an exodus as a person or people leaving a hostile environment. I believe this meaning has largely come from the narrative in the book of Exodus in the Bible. The Greek word translated as *exodus* in the Bible has the simple meaning of a departure or going out.[1] Whenever we journey we are leaving something and going somewhere new. Whether we are leaving a bad place, going into a good place, or simply seeking a change in our life, in all of these, we embark on an exodus.

I have discovered three major journeys we often encounter in life. The first is the journey out of a hostile environment: an abusive relationship, an addiction, hopelessness, and countless other toxic situations that can arise in our lives and often shape us in ways we don't desire.

The second journey is the one out of the status quo. This journey can be needed at various times in life and sometimes more than once. We need to move forward in life because our daily existence is simply becoming too complacent. We know there is more.

There are also times we feel called to step out into a new situation, to live for something bigger than ourselves. This is the third journey—the altruistic journey.

In each of these instances we must depart, exodus, into the unknown future moving toward a promised land.

Each journey ends in finding your promised land. When we apply the principles of Jesus and those found in the Exodus story, our path is smoother, and we find a greater joy in the journey. Your promised land, if you are leaving an addiction, is when you realize the addiction is truly in your past. As you are leaving your status quo, your promised land is that moment you recognize your life has new meaning. As you pursue an altruistic journey, your promised land appears as your calling is fulfilled.

If you are reading this and thinking, w*ell, I'm not really on any of those journeys right now*, that's okay. There is another journey I haven't mentioned. It's easy to miss because it's so obvious—the journey of life. Take two of your outstretched fingers, place them across the bottom of the opposite wrist and see if you detect a pulse. Did you find it? Good stuff! You are alive, and you are already on this journey.

Each of these journeys have many of the same characteristics, pitfalls, and temptations the ancient Israelites faced when they embarked on their

---

1   *Exodos*: pronounced "ex-od-os" means departing or departure; path. Hebrews 11:22 speaks of the exodos of the Israelites from Egypt while Luke 9:31 and 2 Peter 1:15 use the same word translated as "departure."

own journey out of bondage in the Exodus story.[2] Just like we often do when facing the unknown, the Israelites also resisted and wrestled with God concerning their departure.[3] There is so much we can learn from their ancient journey.

You see, God promises our deliverance.[4] The key is, in his wisdom he knows for us to truly *get it* we must truly *go after it*. In other words, God is not a cosmic vending machine. We can't just pop a prayer in and get an instant answer out. It rarely happens that way.

God knows that we must want it, desire it, and be willing to work for it to appreciate it. A profound clue to understanding the basis of this principle can be found in Scripture when God is speaking to his chosen people, the Israelites, through the prophet Jeremiah. "'You will seek me and find me *when you seek me with all your heart*. I will be found by you,' declares the LORD, 'and will bring you back from captivity'" (Jeremiah 29:13-14, emphasis added).

Even though God was speaking to the Israelites, I believe this Scripture can also be applied to our personal lives today and is a basic principle we can apply to many situations.

> ### GUIDING PRINCIPLE: *Seek with All of Your Heart*
>
> God tells us we will find him when we seek him with all of our heart. In Matthew 7:7-9, Jesus tells us if we ask God and seek out the answer, he will open the door. Notice this: the words, *ask* and *seek* are action words. I find that God's answers to prayer often involve me doing the action. The key is, as Jesus says, when we choose the path of action provided by God, the door will open.

Out of a Hostile Environment

In the Exodus story, the Israelites had been in bondage for over 430 years.[5] But God sees their bondage and makes a promise and then lays out their

---

2   Primarily found in Exodus 1-19, but see also Leviticus, Numbers, and Deuteronomy.
3   Exodus 6:6-9
4   Exodus 6:1-8
5   Exodus 1:8-14; 12:40-41

journey out of bondage to the promised land.[6]

In my own life, my childhood started out well. Life was fun. I was ready to tame the world. By the time I was a teen however, I had been burned by the divorce of my parents. I was disillusioned and bitter. So, I figured the best thing to do was simply try to enjoy life and move on, trying to dull the pain. The way I did this was by using drugs. When I was high I was able to live in a world I created in my mind that took away much of the pain. At the time, I thought substances could take away the emotional pain.

I remember telling my mother that God endorses this whole idea of escape. It's okay to smoke marijuana. It allows you to escape the harsher reality of daily living while still maintaining life. I told her to look at what it says in the Bible: "Then God said, 'I give you every seed-bearing plant on the face of the whole earth and every tree that has fruit with seed in it."[7] How can you dispute God's word, I asked her. My mom didn't quite know what to say. The problem was however, that I left out the next sentence in that verse. Those next words add all the truth to God's wisdom: "They will be yours for food."[8]

I was only using God's word to justify my means. I rationalized the solution to my pain in a worldly way and even tried to attribute it to God's wisdom. In my thinking at the time, I simply wanted to smoke pot to escape the reality of my pain every day. Soon I found other stronger substances to help. Cocaine for that great tingly feeling, speed (amphetamines) to make everything seem fun and bright, barbs (barbiturates) to dull the bitterness, PCP to really get way out there, and when I wanted to go on a truly cool vacation, electric Kool-Aid, windowpane, and magic mushrooms (LSD and peyote) to really get away. Of course, cheap wine, beer, and tequila had their place in this grand scheme too. I was up for just about anything.

I thought life was grand and living was cool. My friends and I used to sit in front of the campfire laughing about how we would never make it to forty and what a fun time it would be getting there. Live while the livin's good and be prepared to go out in glory. It's all just a part of the game. Like calling Ralf when you're drinking too much.[9] That's what we thought then anyway.

What I just told you might on the surface sound fun and glorious, but the truth is, I thought I was on a journey then, and though I was, it wasn't the

---

6 Exodus 3:21; 6:6-8
7 Genesis 1:29
8 Genesis 1:29
9 When you've had too much to drink, you lean over the rail or put your head out of the car window and yell, "Raaalllfff!" while expelling everything you've been drinking.

right kind of journey. It was a journey that led to a bondage much like the Israelites in the Exodus story.[10]

As a pastor, I work with many people from many walks of life and see many things, often things I don't want to see. I see women desperately caught up in abusive relationships. The glue often holding them there is a lack of self-worth, the perceived need for love from the person abusing them, acceptance of their status quo, and even the desire to keep the family together for the children. I have helped more than one woman get into a shelter, only to see them leave and go back to their abuser.

Years ago, I met a woman who led a troubled life. When she was seven years old her mother put her and her sisters up for adoption. The family that adopted her abused and tortured her for eight years before they were caught. She then went into the foster care system and ended up in Florida.

Her first husband had a good job working for the city but started doing crack. He ended up farming her out to other men. My friend told me that she didn't like drugs, but she liked beer, so she would dull the pain with beer and more beer to escape. She thought it made it easier to cope. She finally saw some light and got out of this scene by divorcing the guy.

But the pain persisted, and the dulling grind continued as she ended up on the streets. A family member told me once that she was simply drawn to bad men. She got married a second time to another crack head, and the abuse began all over again. Same show, different man.

I met her at a place called Grace and Grits where a hundred or so hungry and homeless people are fed every week. My band would play and entertain as people ate. We would also have a church service every other week after dinner. She would come in with her boyfriend at the time who was also an alcoholic. She would come in all lit up and rosy faced from drinking beer, with a huge smile on her face. In time, we got to know each other, and she started coming to the services after dinner. It was clear she really wanted to journey out of her situation but didn't know where to start.

In both her case, and my own, there was a lot of pain. I dulled my pain with drugs and substances. She dulled her pain with men and beer. Both of us, at these times in our lives, soon found ourselves in over our heads with hopelessness. We were each in need of a journey out; but where to start?

In each of these cases, a journey was desperately needed out of a hostile environment. Maybe you see yourself somewhere in one of these stories or somewhere in between. If so, get your journey shoes on and prepare for your exodus. I left my addiction behind and found my promised land. I know you can find yours too.

Out of the Status Quo

My wife has often told me that her life doesn't have all the contrast mine has. What she means is that for most of her life everything has gone reasonably well with no major pains to deal with, just the day-to-day little junk most people experience. Life never gets too extreme, or too exciting. It's just middle-of-the road, pushing on and wondering if there is more to life than what happens each day.

Each day is filled with the routine. The kids wake up, eat breakfast, and are off to school. The adults go to work for another day of earning the keep, clean the house, do the laundry, and meet the kids after school with a "How was your day?" They head home, have dinner, watch some TV, and go to bed. Then tomorrow it starts all over again.

Maybe your day looks a little like this or nothing like this, but it's still the same thing, day in and day out. Sometimes life just seems redundant. Nothing special, maybe a little drama, but nothing too exciting. Life can sometimes be like an episode of *Father Knows Best*, boring.[11]

Is life so predictable you wonder if you are missing something? It's hard to find true fulfillment in the status quo, isn't it?

We all want our life to have meaning. When we are stuck in the status quo, it's as if all the meaning has been drained out of us and we are simply existing day to day.

Be careful though, the journey out of the status quo could easily lead to the next journey (and that's a good thing): the altruistic journey.

Something Bigger than You

There are times in our lives when we feel a deep and strong compulsion to step into the unknown to quench the inner desires of our hearts. We know there is more. When God calls us to step out in faith into an unknown

---

[11] *Father Knows Best* was a TV show about a family where life was just rosy and went per the status quo. It exemplified the idealized suburban family of the 1950s.

future, this is what we call the altruistic journey.[12]

As a young man, I too felt this deep longing for God. It all started with my grandmother taking me to church each Sunday as a toddler since my parents didn't go at the time. As I grew my parents started to become more involved in church and we would go together, and they taught Sunday School.

As I entered my teen years however, my parent's relationship started to fall apart. Their involvement in my spiritual life started falling away so I struck out on my own to seek God and take ownership of my faith. For a time, I felt deeply that God was with me and wanted me to do something. I didn't know what that something was, though I did know it involved loving others.

The bottom fell out when my parents divorced. I was fourteen. It threw my life in disarray. I lost sight of God's calling in my heart. This was when I started trying to manage the clutter with substances claiming to help me escape.

I went in the service at 19 years old, right out of high school, in 1974. I was chasing a girl I was in love with whose family had moved from Virginia to Georgia, so I signed up to be stationed at Ft. Benning to be near her.

This first leg of my military service was not an altruistic journey, but I need to share it here for you to grasp the full impact of God later down the path. As you will see, God used this time in my life to bring me out of my addiction.

During this time in my life, I wasn't listening to God. In addition, the girl I joined the Army to be near broke my heart when she married someone else. As I look back, I guess I can't blame her. I was no catch. I only thought of myself, my decisions were only for me, and I was an addict. I also hated the Army and my substance abuse was getting even worse.

I loved the adventure the Army gave me but hated the discipline. In my mind the Army controlled me. They controlled what I said and how I said it, they controlled how I looked, they controlled everything I did. I didn't have a girlfriend anymore, and I certainly felt like I didn't have a life anymore, so, I did my three years, got out, and was thrilled.

Five years down the line, life just kept getting worse. I had gotten married on a whim and divorced not long after. My relationships were a mess. I didn't understand myself, and jobs were not easy to get or keep. I was losing everything, darkness was winning. I spent every day getting high on whatever I could find.

---

12 Altruism: "unselfish regard for or devotion to the welfare of others." *Merriam-Webster*, s.v. "altruism," accessed March 15, 2018, www.merriam-webster.com/dictionary/altruism

At this point I could see that drugs were not dulling the pain as much as they were causing it. This was the pain from a life devoid of hope. The drugs were now controlling my life. I tried many times to stop. I even moved from Melbourne, Florida to Daytona beach (A party town, go figure!) so I could start anew and get away from my druggie friends in Melbourne. But Daytona Beach and working on the boardwalk is no place to go to get away from drugs. I had tried so many times to stop but nothing worked. Every day ended up being a substance filled party.

In the night however, I started crying out to God in the deep and lonely recesses of my soul. I could hardly take care of myself. I knew my dreams of a wife and family were slipping away. Why? All my relationships were based on sex, drugs, and rock and roll. Not a pretty picture for someone who set out to tame the world and wanted a family more than anything else.

But in 1983 things started to change. It was clear *my* way was leading me nowhere, so I tried asking God to lead the way. I started listening to him and doing things his way instead of my and the world's way. I began to surrender my deeply scarred heart to God.

Then, as an answer to prayer and my crying out, I started to hear this still small voice. It eventually got loud, yelling at me saying, "Go back in the Army you fool! If you can't make it there you won't make it anywhere!"

Miraculously, in six months, I was able to accomplish what I had tried to accomplish so many times in the previous five years. I got clean. I was able to rid my body of all the substances so I could pass a drug test. My altruistic journey had now begun.

This time, joined by the master journey guide, Jesus, I went back into the Army, proudly serving both God and country. I retired in 1997 with medals on my chest. During this second time in the Army, God taught me to live for a greater purpose than myself. I also received another great gift from God. I was blessed to meet and marry a wonderful woman with whom my dreams of a family and love would come true.

Something More

During this whole time, from when I got clean to when I retired from the Army, I knew I was still searching for something. I knew Jesus was with me, but I knew something was still missing in my life. God had blessed my family and our life, and while I wasn't sure what it was, I knew there was more.

In 2002 my family and I went to a new church. I started to get involved, serving anywhere and everywhere I was needed. If the doors were open, I wanted to be there. A year later, I sat down with my wife and said, "Honey, I need to talk to you. I feel like God is calling me to be a pastor."

In a similar way, I have friends who felt called to be police officers, missionaries, school teachers, soldiers, firemen, airmen, and sailors.

The common thread I see here is the calling is not done for money or reward. A calling like this is done for a deeper purpose, one of living for something that is greater than we are.

Come One Come All: Making the Decision to Go

Each of these three journeys happen in our lives at one time or another. Sometimes they even happen at the same time. The truth is, they are all part of life.

We all want to be successful in life's journey. No one is guaranteed an easy road, but with Jesus at our side we find the route easier to navigate. Whether you are on a journey out of a bad place, out of the status quo, or an altruistic one, my hope is that as you read this book you will discover principles and avoid pitfalls which can threaten to take away your hope of success on the journey. Are you ready to go?

2
Getting Ready to Go

Thinking well is wise, planning well is wiser, but doing well is wisest.
—Ancient Persian Proverb

And do this, understanding the present time:
The hour has already come for you to wake up from your slumber, because our salvation is nearer now than when we first believed.

— Romans 13:11

Like any journey we embark on, before we depart, we must always prepare. We prepare by assembling the tools, supplies, and mind we will need to navigate the path before us. In this chapter I want to introduce you to the attitudes that Jesus tells us will result in blessing. They are the most important tools we need to successfully navigate the path before us toward our promised land.

Maya Angelou, poet, singer, and civil rights activist, shared, "For me, the Bible is a map in the hands of a person about to take a journey. This map will show you every stop; it will show you the oases; it will help you see where you can get water; you will find out where you can get sustenance; it is the atlas of life!"[13]

The Attitudes of our Life

No matter what kind of journey we are on, Jesus is our guide. So, what better place to start, than to ask his advice, right?

Jesus starts out his greatest discourse in Scripture, the Sermon on the Mount, with the most amazing detail.[14] As Jesus is teaching his disciples on the mountainside, he starts by speaking about attitudes in life; eight positive attitudes that change lives. These are called the Beatitudes. They are such great, beautiful attitudes on how we can be. These attitudes may be the most important part of preparing to start our journey and for what is ahead. Listen to what Jesus said:

> Blessed are the poor in spirit,
>   for theirs is the kingdom of heaven.
> Blessed are those who mourn,
>   for they will be comforted.
> Blessed are the meek,
>   for they will inherit the earth.
> Blessed are those who hunger and thirst for righteousness,
>   for they will be filled.

---

13 *The Bible: The Epic Miniseries.* "Extras: Believing in Miracles." Disc 4. Directed by Crispin Reese, Tony Mitchell, Christopher Spencer. Twentieth Century Fox, April 8, 2014.
14 Matthew 5-7

> Blessed are the merciful,
> > for they will be shown mercy.
> Blessed are the pure in heart,
> > for they will see God.
> Blessed are the peacemakers,
> > for they will be called children of God.
> Blessed are those who are persecuted because of righteousness,
> > for theirs is the kingdom of heaven. (Matthew 5:3-10)

Stop for a moment and ponder how you might start to apply these attitudes to your journey and to your life. These attitudes are tools that can help guide and carry us through the many twists and forks in the road ahead.

Jesus Speaks the Truth Upside-Down

Our journeys and our lives build on the foundation of these truths from the Beatitudes. These eight attitudes are full of paradox, the opposite of what the world would have us think, and when these truths are applied, they grab us and shake us up.

As you look at these attitudes, on the surface they may seem a little cryptic or hard to understand. To understand this wisdom, it is important that we first understand the context of what the listeners were hearing when Jesus spoke in that day.

> **GUIDING PRINCIPLE : *The Truth is Often Upside-Down***
>
> The truth of Jesus is full of paradox. His truth often seems absurd, but it is always full of wisdom. Something deeply spiritual happens when we apply this wisdom to our lives. Let the upside-down truth and wisdom of Jesus be your guide.

We must not look at the Beatitudes solely on their own. They are the very beginning of the larger context of The Sermon on the Mount. When I preach, I would never expect someone to fully understand my sermon after only hearing the first five minutes. In his book, *The Message of the Sermon on the Mount,* John Stott shares with us the purpose of Jesus' discourse, "it is his own description of what he wanted his followers to be and to do."[15] Jesus ends the Sermon on the Mount with these words:

> Therefore everyone who hears these words of mine and puts them into practice is like a wise man who built his house on the rock. The rain came down, the streams rose, and the winds blew and beat against that house; yet it did not fall, because it had its foundation on the rock. But everyone who hears these words of mine and does not put them into practice is like a foolish man who built his house on sand. The rain came down, the streams rose, and the winds blew and beat against that house, and it fell with a great crash. (Matthew 7:24-27)

Today so many people ask the question, "What can Jesus do for me?" Yet what Jesus ultimately wants is for us to do for others. In the Beatitudes, his listeners heard how to start *being*, so they could now *do*.

Can We Live Up to This Standard?

As we look at and begin to understand the Beatitudes, we may start to feel like we can never live up to this standard. Some scholars have even dismissed the Beatitudes as an impossible ideal or standard to reach. What I believe they don't understand, however, is that the Beatitudes are attitudes we adopt and build into our lives, not final goals we somehow reach.

Thankfully, with Jesus, it is never about being perfect.[16] All he wants from us is to trust him, take the guidance he offers, and grow. If we could see these attitudes playing out in our life in real time, they may look like the bands on a graphic equalizer. I developed a little tool called the Beatilizer (beatitude equalizer) to help illustrate this:

---

15 John R. W. Stott *The Message of the Sermon on the Mount – (Matthew 5-7 : Christian Counter-Culture)* (Downers Grove: InterVarsity Press, 1985), 14–15.
16 As I looked at the many Greek words Jesus used and translated as "perfect," I saw one thing in common, they are all described using action words, "to make," "to carry through," "to add what is yet wanting." This suggests perfection is a path or journey, not a final destination.

If you were to look at these eight attitudes as they are playing out at any moment in your life, they might look like the Beatilizer pictured here. Can you see how it looks like the bands on a graphic equalizer? The higher the band (small blocks), the stronger the attitude. Conversely, the lower the band, the more that attitude is lacking. Look at any moment in your life and one attitude might be stronger than another, or one attitude may be needing some attention. Our humanness makes it so. This little tool is a helpful way for you to visualize how these attitudes are either thriving or not thriving in your life.

When I was younger and still did not understand what a relationship with Jesus was, my Beatilizer looked like the one above. Notice the poor in spirit band; it's pretty low. I was still trying to live life on my own wisdom. I did not fully trust God and had not surrendered my heart to him. The mourning band is also low. Even if I recognized the sin in my life, I paid it little mind.

Let's look at the other bands (attitudes): the meekness band is a little higher and so is the righteousness band. I still had a long way to go in trusting God, however, and though I was a good person, my heart was anything but pure (pure in heart). I only thought of myself and when angered, I often sought retribution or revenge. I just wanted to get back at someone who wronged me (being a peacemaker). I often had a hard time understanding life and let other people's words and actions affect me. I was very conscious and wary of being persecuted. I didn't want to be made fun of for being a Christian and allowed that to shape me rather than getting my strength through Christ (persecuted for righteousness).

> **GUIDING PRINCIPLE:**
> *Perfection is a Journey, Not a Destination*
> Very often we feel we cannot measure up. If we recognize that Jesus works in our weakness and we are on a path to perfection with Him, then we can see hope in our lives.

Each of these eight attitudes ends with a state of blessedness. Blessedness is not necessarily happiness, and it is not a gift for doing the right thing. It is also not something to be earned or presented to us. Blessedness is an experience of hope and joy. It is independent of our outward actions. Blessedness is the beauty that overflows from applying God's wisdom to our lives.

It is important to point out these eight attitudes can be applied to most of the situations we face, whether a simple question of honesty or the struggles and troubles we face in life. As we discuss each beatitude, I will present them as they apply to a journey. In Appendix 1, I provide more examples, so you can get a fuller picture of how they can be applied to any situation you face in life. Our journey in life is not about the quantity of miles we walk, it is about the quality of our daily walk. As we embark on our journeys, these attitudes will guide us to blessing; they help us reach our promised land.

Finally, let me point out the genius of Jesus and God's wisdom. These attitudes are presented in an order; each attitude building on the previous ones until we get to a point of great harmony. At the same time, we should not approach these attitudes as needing to get one right before moving on to the next but recognize that as we work on each one they build and grow together. More specifically, the first five attitudes build our hearts and strengthen our life experience, and the last three attitudes are largely the result of the application of the first five. Jesus is amazing!

Before we move ahead, let's take another look at the Beatitudes as Jesus spoke them. I want you to read them through slowly. Focus on each one as you read. Read them once, read them twice, really focus on them, and read them again. Then, in the next two chapters, we will look closely at each specific attitude; what it means, and how each one can apply as we journey in life. Listen again to the amazing words of Jesus:

> Blessed are the poor in spirit,
> for theirs is the kingdom of heaven.
> Blessed are those who mourn,
> for they will be comforted.
> Blessed are the meek,
> for they will inherit the earth.
> Blessed are those who hunger and thirst for righteousness,
> for they will be filled.
> Blessed are the merciful,
> for they will be shown mercy.
> Blessed are the pure in heart,
> for they will see God.
> Blessed are the peacemakers,
> for they will be called children of God.
> Blessed are those who are persecuted because of righteousness,
> for theirs is the kingdom of heaven. (Matthew 5:3-10)

3
Attitudes That Build Our Hearts:
THE BLESSED ATTITUDES

"It is only when we can see where we've been and see where we are, we can finally see where we need to go."

Finally, brothers and sisters, whatever is true, whatever is noble, whatever is right, whatever is pure, whatever is lovely, whatever is admirable—if anything is excellent or praiseworthy— think about such things.

— Philippians 4:8

Before we can fully plan for a journey we have to be in the right mental state. Our attitudes affect our behavior. Good attitudes help us make good decisions. They guide our work ethic and give us untold strength. Wrong attitudes (not necessarily bad ones) do the same, but in a negative manner. Sometimes we don't even recognize when these negative attitudes have claimed a stake in our lives. When this happens, what are we to do?

In chapter 2 we spent time looking at the Beatitudes as a whole. In the next two chapters we'll take a closer look at each of these eight heart attitudes Jesus has shared with us. First, we will look at the Beatitudes that build our hearts in ways that strengthen our lives. Then, in chapter 4 we will look at the Beatitudes that guide our hearts.

The Blessed Attitudes

The first five attitudes Jesus shares from his Sermon on the Mount, build our hearts in ways that strengthen our lives. When we start internalizing, applying, and working through these first attitudes, a change starts to take place inside us and our hearts are guided towards the promised land bringing joy and fulfillment to our lives. These attitudes are ones we can intentionally work on in our hearts.

"Blessed are the Poor in Spirit, for Theirs is the Kingdom of Heaven."

This first beatitude may seem a little cryptic. In fact, it hits me squarely in the forehead getting my attention when I read it! What does it mean to be poor in spirit? The poor in spirit are those who are utterly dependent on God. They are those who are humble in spirit as opposed to relying on themselves and having no need for God.

The world recognizes self-reliance, self-confidence, and self-direction as virtues. However, when we live by the world's wisdom, all the pressure is on us to complete the journey. But as we submit to God's will, rather than our own, and admit our dependence on Him, the pressure is no longer ours. We can free ourselves from worry like "the birds of the air," because we know that God will provide what we need on the journey.[17]

As you ponder this absence of self-pride in the face of God, giving him

---

17 Matthew 6:26

more control of your life, remember, like so many things, this is a process. This is especially important in the instant gratification world we live in today. It's easy to want something, and to want it to happen now, but I promise you, these attitudes are worth the process.

> **GUIDING PRINCIPLE:** *Pray the Hard Prayer*
>
> It is easy to pray for the outcome we desire. God is the creator of life. He knows us inside and out. Ultimately, I want what God knows is best for me over what I think is best. The hard prayer usually goes something like this: "Lord, open the door if it is what you want for me. Close the door if this is not. I trust you." You can also pray, "Give me the strength to do what is right in your eyes, not what I think is best for myself." If you have a tough time surrendering your will to God or trusting in his wisdom, ask specifically for that: "Lord, help me surrender my will, help me trust in Your wisdom."

When I first enlisted in the Army and was in basic training, the drill sergeants did something that was counter-intuitive, but so wise. They tore us down to build us up. They did this so we could learn from scratch and be built up into soldiers and leaders. Their goal was to change our way of thinking by introducing a new way, and to ensure our survival on the battlefield. We had to basically forget and discard almost all we had been previously taught about our self-centered ways and our know-it-all attitudes. This allowed us to be receptive to the truth of their ways and training, so we would be best prepared for battle. In their own simple way, our drill sergeants taught us to be "poor in spirit." It worked!

Miles J. Stanford, a Christian author best known for his classic collection on spirituality says, "In preparation, there is a tearing down before there can be a building up."[18] The prophet Hosea tells us, "Come, let us return to the LORD; for he has torn us, that he may heal us; he has struck us down, and he will bind us up."[19] Ask God for guidance and for the strength to allow you to trust totally in him. Realize each day you wrestle with this, you will become stronger.

18 M.J. Standford, *The Complete Green Letters* (Grand Rapids: Zondervan, 1983), 19.
19 Hosea 6:1 (ESV)

I want to point out that the attitude of being poor in spirit, of relying totally on God, is an intellectual attitude. We can choose intellectually to follow the world's wisdom, our own wisdom, or to seek and submit to God's wisdom.

The Exodus story provides a fitting example of what it means to be poor in spirit. In Exodus 3:11 God tells Moses that Moses will lead the Israelites out of bondage from Egypt. How does Moses reply? He questions his own ability and says, "Who am I that I should go to Pharaoh and bring the Israelites out of Egypt?" But God answers Moses, telling him, "I will be with you" (v. 12).

In 2003 I felt strongly called to pastoral ministry. I remember many times talking to my wife in tears asking, "Who am I to be called into ministry? I haven't led the best life. I am in my 40's. I don't have a strong Biblical education." But my wife encouraged me to keep moving ahead. I could hear God's voice in the background saying, "I will be with you."

It was a full five years before I was ordained. It took a long time, but I trusted God. I surrendered to his will and studied. Most of all, I applied the heart of God in my life by serving the elderly, the poor, and people in need around me. It wasn't easy, but it was humbling and rewarding. Even today, I can hear God's quiet voice inside saying, "Don't worry, I am here with you."

Many years ago, I was helping a young mother who was in recovery to rely on Jesus. At 14 years old her own mother had taught her to shoot up oxycodone. Her whole family had a long history of substance abuse. I spent a great amount of time helping her.

One day while she was in rehab she told me, "Pastor Jan, I kneel on a towel by my bed every day and pray asking Jesus to help me, just like you told me, but I just don't feel his presence." I remember telling her maybe she was just trying too hard, and to try to let go and simply trust.

Soon after that, she got out of rehab and was renting a room from a friend of mine. She had a job, but her car broke down beyond repair. She called me, worried and panicking she wouldn't be able to find a new car and would lose her job. I told her to have faith; Jesus didn't bring her this far to let her fall. We knew all these things in her life were helping her stay clean and now they were being threatened. She needed a car to keep the job to pay the rent, which would be instrumental in keeping her from giving up and ending up back on the street, likely relapsing.

But here is what is important: After she told me her car was beyond repair and she had no money, she said to me with quiet peace and confidence, "Pastor Jan, I just need to trust Jesus." I remember thinking that finally, she was understanding what it meant to rely on God and not herself. I also remember thinking, *Now, where are we gonna find a car? That's a tall order!*

I told our church administrative assistant about our dilemma and she said, "Put a request on Facebook." *Yeah right,* I thought, *but who am I to limit God?* So we went ahead and put the request on Facebook. Less than an hour later a woman in our congregation commented she had an old, yet well running Honda Civic that had just been sitting in her driveway. Long story short, this young mother in need had a working car two days later!

As we embark on our own journeys, we must rely on Jesus through every turn, every obstacle, and every step of the way. If we think we can get to our destination on our own, we probably won't. If we think we have the answers, we probably don't. We can't do it alone. Without God's love, wisdom and guidance, we are nothing and we can't reach the destination he wants for us.

What is the blessing of trusting and depending on Jesus throughout our journey? Jesus tells us "theirs is the kingdom of heaven."[20] I find this fact amazing. Jesus is telling us that life, not death, is the beginning of our journey into the kingdom of heaven when we trust in him and depend on Him. More on that later. Let's move to the next beatitude:

"Blessed are Those Who Mourn, for they Will be Comforted."

On the surface there seems to be a contradiction here. Mourning doesn't seem to equate blessing at all. We often associate mourning with death. You might ask, "Well Pastor Jan, how can someone who is mourning be blessed?" You see, the mourning Jesus is talking about here has nothing to do with death, but everything to do with the sin in your life and this world.

Have you ever told a lie because you felt it benefited you? Did you recognize that telling that lie was wrong regardless of the outcome? When you are caught in it you feel pain, right? How about stealing from work or cheating on your taxes? Many people do these things and do not recognize them as sin, or even as being wrong, if we seem to benefit in some way.

But God knows us inside and out. He tells us about sin and what it is because he knows it hurts us and breaks our relationships. Even when we think we are helping ourselves by sinning, we aren't. When we start to see how our sin wreaks havoc (enslaving us to an endless circle of pain and suffering in life), and as we start to see the depth of the suffering in the world, it starts to break our heart. This is the mourning Jesus is talking about.

20 Matthew 5:3

Mourning is also part of the process of repentance (a biblical word basically meaning to turn the opposite direction from our sin).

As humans, we can easily get caught up in hating our sin and transferring that hate onto ourselves for sinning. But Jesus wants us to simply recognize our sin and turn from it. Jesus is not calling for self-loathing, hating yourself, or disliking who you are. Jesus knows it is only when we can see the sin, and the slow, often veiled suffering it brings, that we can find true fulfillment through the comfort of God.

This second attitude addresses the same issues of trusting and depending on God as the first one, but from more of an emotional perspective rather than an intellectual one. As you emotionally recognize your dependence on God, you start to see yourself, and many things in the world, in a different light and are more able to face whatever the journey brings.

Finally, Jesus tells us that when we mourn the sin in our lives it will result in blessing: "For they will be comforted." God wants to deliver you. He wants to be there for you and with you on this journey. It is only when we can see where we've been and see where we are, we can finally see where we need to go. As you mourn the sin in your life, cry out to God for forgiveness and ask for deliverance. He *will* hear your cry just as he heard the cry of the Israelites in Egypt.[21]

Each Beatitude Builds on Itself: As we learn to trust God (the poor in spirit), to fully trust Jesus in our lives and to become utterly dependent on Him, we will find it easier to see the sin in our lives and to mourn it. I have found healing in clearly identifying my sin and mourning it.

People who depend on God have an incredible ability to face with joy whatever their journey brings, because they know that Jesus is with them. Let's look at the next beatitude:

"Blessed Are the Meek, for They Will Inherit the Earth."

As we seek to internalize these beautiful attitudes the next building block is the attitude of meekness. This too hits us squarely in the forehead because it seems to counter what we have been taught. The world's wisdom tells us in order to embark on life's journey we must be strong, powerful, and in control of our destiny; yet Jesus is saying to be meek.

You may be wondering, isn't being meek the same thing as weakness? These two traits are actually very different. Let me share with you another

---

21 Exodus 2:23-25

example of the upside-down truth of Jesus. The Greek word translated here as "meek" is *praus* (pronounced prah-ooce) meaning "humble" or "gentle." Weakness, on the contrary, is a lack of strength. So, weakness is lacking strength, while meekness is having strength under control.

Meekness is not always being defensive. Meekness is not having to flaunt your strength or always be right. Meekness is not feeling like you are above or better than others. Meekness is strength in humility. Think of it like an airplane wing. The wings are strong, yet flexible and light. If they weren't these things, the plane would never leave the ground. As we come to understand true meekness, we will see a strength and flexibility of character envelop our journey as well as our life.

I searched the Scriptures and could only find two people described as meek. These two people are probably not who you would think or expect. They are Moses and Jesus.

Yes, Moses, who stood up to Pharaoh and led God's people out of the bondage of slavery to the promised land in Exodus. He exemplified great courage and leadership. The Bible says he was the meekest of all men on earth.[22]

Jesus, the greatest of all men, God in the flesh, who leads us out of the bondage of sin, who willingly died on the cross for you and me, this Jesus, is meek.[23] Jesus knew he was facing certain death as he prayed in the garden of Gethsemane, yet he walked forward to the cross out of obedience to God and love for us.[24]

Jesus was gentle, humble, and kind. He exhibited tremendous courage while confronting the religious authorities who sought to trap him. He had the courage to drive the money changers out of the temple who were desecrating it by their trade.[25] On the way to the cross he had the strength and control, to reprimand Peter (who was simply protecting Jesus from the authorities) for cutting off the ear of one of the high priests servants.[26] This, my friend, is not weakness.

The blessing that Jesus imparts here is another slightly cryptic one to the modern mind: "For they will inherit the earth." In Jewish thought, the earth was more than just the planet we live on. It was the whole of our outer experience. What the listener in Jesus' day heard when he said this

---

22 Numbers 12:3
23 Matthew 11:29 (KJV)
24 Mathew 26:39
25 Matthew 21:12-13
26 Luke 22:49-51

was that the meek would inherit the promised land, a place of true harmony and success.

As you are on your journey, whether it be heading out of a bad place, out of the status quo, or because you have been called to live for something bigger than yourself, the desire is to reach the *promised land*. As believers we know that eventually we will inherit a new heaven and a new earth.[27] In the Old Testament, David shares this same thought in the Psalms, "But the meek will inherit the land and enjoy peace and prosperity."[28]

Each Beatitude Builds on Itself: Notice how it is hard to be meek if you are self-made and self-reliant. We must rely on Jesus to find strength in meekness (the poor in spirit). It is also not easy to be meek unless we can see ourselves as we truly are (those who mourn). We must see our sin for what it is and then we can act on the strength of our character in meekness, kindness, grace, and gentleness. In other words, as we learn to trust in Jesus and honestly see the sin in our lives, it is easier to be meek.

"Blessed Are Those Who Hunger and Thirst for Righteousness, for They Will Be Filled."

Finally! Jesus shares an attitude that is easier for our modern minds. First, what is righteousness? Righteousness is simply living in accordance with the moral and ethical standards of God—doing what it right. Sounds pretty simple doesn't it? Yet, how often are we faced with the temptation of relief from pain in the guise of pleasure, only to find later that it enslaves us?

And notice this, Jesus not only says to do what is right, but he says we should *hunger and thirst* for it.[29] There is an inherent strength in doing what is right. When we hunger and thirst to do what is right, we can hardly be wrong. Seek out the right course of action—righteousness—through Scripture, prayer, and wise counsel, and then take action. Become doers of the Word, not just listeners.[30]

It doesn't matter what journey you are on, if you truly want to arrive in the promised land, it is best to always seek God's path and not try to take shortcuts.

---

27 Revelation 21:1-4
28 Psalms 37:11
29 Matthew 5:6
30 James 1:21-22

> **GUIDING PRINCIPLE:** *God Can't Bless That Which Is Wrong*
> If you want God's blessing, which we all do, we must make decisions in line with his principles: honesty and integrity, decisions that are morally sound, and to love God and your neighbor as yourself (Leviticus 19:18 and Mark 12:31). A good parent would never bless their child for stealing a car, cheating on a test, lying to get a job, or hurting someone to get ahead. God is also our father. He can't bless that which is wrong.

Let's look at the blessed result of hungering and thirsting for righteousness. The Greek word translated as "filled," is *chortazo* (pronounced khor-tad-zo). Chortazo means "to be satisfied." Isn't that what we all want in life?

When we do what is right, when we live in accordance with moral standards, Jesus promises that we will be filled with righteousness. When we seek to do the right things in life we are feeding our soul and we will be filled with God's grace, we will be satisfied. This is contrary to what the world tells us when it says to pursue happiness at any cost.

Each Beatitude Builds on Itself: I talk to people all the time who make decisions that are not morally grounded, but they accept them as the right thing to do. To *truly* understand the right thing to do, we must be in a place where we first depend on Jesus and recognize our need for Him (poor in spirit). We must first see ourselves and our sin for what it is (mourning). We must be humble (meekness) enough to recognize sin and seek to change it. At this point we are ready to understand God's concepts of righteousness.

I pray that you are starting to see the amazing genius of Jesus. Would we expect anything less from the author of life?

"Blessed are the Merciful, for they Will be Shown Mercy."

What exactly is mercy? Mercy is best understood by understanding its relationship to grace. Grace is a pardon, an immunity from the effects of something. Grace is usually associated with having done something wrong. God granted us grace. We didn't deserve it, but God gave it.

Mercy, however, is different. I like to say that mercy, especially in the biblical sense, is grace in action. God granted us grace, and then, in mercy, came to earth as a human—Jesus—and died a terrible death on the cross so we might be free from the penalty of sin. Remarkably, when Jesus was on the cross, enduring unimaginable suffering, he extended mercy to those who put him there. He also showed mercy to the thief hanging beside him, by granting forgiveness.[31] Mercy is exercising grace.

How does mercy play out on our journey and in our lives? Grace is feeling compassion for someone's situation. Mercy is helping to do something about it. Grace is empathizing with someone's pain or suffering. Mercy is stepping in to help alleviate that pain or suffering.

The word for mercy translated from the Greek is *eleeo* (pronounced "el-eh-eh-o"). It means "to have compassion" and is always an action. It is not just feeling deep sympathy for someone's situation, it is also having an active desire to help the situation.

The blessing that comes from showing mercy is that we will receive what we have sown: mercy. At this point in our attitude journey, we are ready to understand the heart behind the saying, "you reap what you sow" (which is often used in a negative way, though it doesn't need to be).[32] Jesus tells us when we have a heart attitude of what we extend to others (when we sow mercy)—we will also have mercy extended to us (we will reap mercy).

Each Beatitude Builds on Itself: This attitude is best understood as we have come to a place of depending deeply on God (poor in spirit) and understanding what it means to mourn the sin in our life. It takes humility to be merciful (meekness) and it is certainly the right thing to do (hungering for righteousness). Our sin separated us from God, but God showed us mercy. Jesus died so we might be free from the penalty for sin (eternal death). While there are consequences for our sin, Jesus' death on the cross paid for it. God showed us mercy.

In the next chapter we will look at the remaining three attitudes and will explore how they guide our hearts.

---

31 Luke 23:34,43
32 Galatians 6:7; Proverbs 11:18

4
Attitudes That Guide Our Hearts:
THE STRENGTH WITHIN YOU

"People are like stained-glass windows.
They sparkle and shine when the sun is out,
but when the darkness sets in,
their true beauty is revealed
only if there is a light from within."

— Elizabeth Kübler-Ross

Do not conform to the pattern of this world,
but be transformed by the renewing of your mind.

— Romans 12:2

We have looked at five attitudes we can apply to our lives with intentionality:

1. Blessed are the poor in spirit
2. Blessed are those who mourn
3. Blessed are the meek
4. Blessed are those who hunger and thirst for righteousness
5. Blessed are the merciful

As we look at the last three attitudes, we will see the results that come when we apply the first five. At this point in our attitude journey, something is happening deep inside of us as a result of applying these first five attitudes. Our hearts are changing.

"Blessed Are the Pure in Heart, for They Will See God."

It's easy to think that being pure in heart implies being sinless. We may think this way because we are prone to believing the world we live in is black and white, instead of one with many different shades. The truth is however, that purity in heart is a process, not a state of being.

So what does it mean to be pure in heart if it does not mean being sinless? It means being *inwardly* clean in the secret recesses of our heart. It means being biblically moral and honest; to show mercy to others and to depend wholly on God. It means to live without hypocrisy. When we are pure in heart, we have one purpose—to glorify God—in all that we do.

I read once about a woman who was effectively blind from birth. She could only see blurs and outlines, nothing was in focus. As an adult, a surgeon was able to operate on her eyes and restore her sight. The newspaper reported, "she found that everything was 'so much bigger and brighter' than she ever imagined."[33]

In the same way, when we adopt these attitudes in our lives, our sight is restored. Everything is bigger, brighter, and more robust. Life comes into focus as we start to see with much more clarity. Jesus promised it when he said, "they will see God."[34]

I think this is what Helen Keller meant when someone bluntly said to her, "Isn't it terrible to be blind?" She responded, "Better to be blind and see with

---

33 R. Kent Hughes, *The Sermon on the Mount: The Message of the Kingdom, Preaching the Word* (Wheaton, IL: Crossway Books, 2001), 53.
34 Matthew 5:8

your heart, than to have two good eyes and see nothing."[35]

While it is possible for some of the previous attitudes to be imitated, purity of heart cannot. In my own life, I have, by far, not achieved any of these attitudes perfectly. But as I have made every effort to apply them in my life, my heart has begun to change. When I fall, which I do at times, I get back up and try again. Adopting and applying the Beatitudes to our life is a process and part of our journey and as we apply them, our heart begins to purify.

Next, let's look at the blessing, "for they will see God." As you start to apply these attitudes in your life, and as your heart changes, you start to see out of what I call, *God glasses*. These are glasses that help you see people as God sees people—with love, compassion, and empathy. Even more so, we can also see his footsteps beside us as we look back on our lives. What a wonderful view it is to see through our God glasses whether we are high on a mountain or deep in a valley. We can look back to see the beauty of where God has been. Seeing God's presence in our lives certainly gives us strength to know that not only has he been with us, but that he will continue to be as we move ahead.

> *GUIDING PRINCIPLE: Want to See God? Keep Looking Back.*
>
> People sometimes tell me they have a hard time seeing God in their lives. I often tell them they are probably looking in the wrong direction. The upside-down truth is that we cannot see God head on, but we can see where he has been. In Exodus 33:18-23, Moses asks to see God's glory. God replies that Moses would not be allowed to see his face. However, God told Moses he would place him in the cleft of a rock and after he passed by, Moses would be able to see his back. Here is the key: As you come closer in relationship to God and see his movement in your life, you will naturally know his presence is with you and indeed, know he is there.

Each Beatitude Builds on Itself: When we recognize that we need God for everything concerning our lives (poor in spirit), when we mourn our sin (those who mourn) , when we start to find that strength of character to humble ourselves before God and others (the meek), when we hunger

---

35 Hughes, *The Sermon on the Mount: The Message of the Kingdom, Preaching the Word*, 57.

and thirst to know and do what is right (hungering and thirsting for righteousness) and when we show mercy to others—we experience inner cleansing in our hearts. This *process* is purity in heart.

"Blessed Are the Peacemakers, for They Will Be Called Children of God."

The Greek word translated as peacemakers is *eirenopoios*, (pronounced i-ray-nop-oy-os) and it means "someone who loves peace," or "reconciler."

In the Old Testament the Hebrew word for peace is *shalom* (pronounced shaw-lome). It was, and still is, a Jewish greeting meaning, peace, tranquility, and contentment.

So what does it look like to be someone who loves peace, to be a reconciler, and to be at peace? At times we find ourselves in situations where we want to strike out in anger. There are also times our paths are crossed with those who are in deep conflict with themselves or with others. When we find ourselves in these moments lashing out in return would be the easy and natural response. But, there is great blessing in taking the high ground and seeking to reconcile peace in the hearts of ourselves and others.

We often struggle in relationship with people at work, neighbors, or people we encounter. If we are not careful, these relationships can sour, and we start to forget they can be mended. Who will take the first step in establishing peace? Who will throw away the invisible scorecard tracking the wrongs inflicted? This is what a peacemaker does. We are called to be peacemakers.

It's easy to feel somewhat stuck when we find ourselves in these situations, as if there is no hope. But there is hope. Throw away your scorecard and be the peacemaker. (God threw away his scorecard on us through Jesus because he is the ultimate peacemaker.) Start doing positive things for these people in your life, like taking them to lunch, surprising them with a kind and honest thought, a card, a small gift, do the things that seek peace between you and them. I am happy to report that when I do these things, relationships often get better and peace is made. It's a process, but it is a beautiful God ordained process. Be the peacemaker.

Even when you are a peacemaker, there will always be people who will want to reflect their pain on you, whether intentionally or not, and refuse to live in peace. While this can be difficult, as you have now started to internalize and apply the attitudes we have been discussing, you will have the strength in your character to face these situations and people with compassion.

The point here is that if someone wants to be angry with you, let it be for doing the right thing and not for the wrong thing. Let it be because of your righteousness and pure heart, not because of any wrong you have done to them.

Finally, it doesn't surprise me one bit the blessing which comes from this attitude is: "they will be called children of God." When we live as a peacemaker, we are seeking to do what God does—love people with his love. As we see ourselves as a child of God, our self-worth becomes stronger. Like a child, when we feel stable and secure in who we are, we can easily focus on the needs of others; we are less defensive, less fearful, kinder, and more forgiving—we make peace.

Each Beatitude Builds on Itself: As we fully trust God to help us make peace (poor in spirit), as we see our own shortcomings (mourning) and humbly love others in conflict (meekness), as we hunger to help those in conflict (hunger and thirst for righteousness), as we show mercy to those around us, an inner cleansing process begins to take hold in our lives (the pure in heart). We start to desire to mend our relationships with others rather than simply accept the brokenness of the relationship.

"Blessed Are Those Who Are Persecuted Because of Righteousness, for Theirs Is the Kingdom of Heaven."

This one sounds tough, doesn't it? Especially since it's pretty much a given that no one wants to be persecuted. So, how can we have joy when being persecuted? The qualifying thought here is "because of righteousness."[36]

In this attitude, Jesus goes on to immediately expound on this thought of persecution. He says, "Blessed are you when people insult you, persecute you and falsely say all kinds of evil against you because of me. Rejoice and be glad, because great is your reward in heaven, for in the same way they persecuted the prophets who were before you."[37]

What does persecution look like? I have a friend who was heavily ridiculed by many colleagues in his office for choosing to listen to sermons through his headphones instead of listening to the vulgar office music they played. He was doing this on his own and not intending to bring attention to it, but a co-worker who was sitting behind him overheard and said, "It's not Sunday man! I'm tired of hearing God this and God that through your headphones!" My friend apologized for the volume and said he'd turn it down. He heard laughing a couple of minutes later and looked up to see several people doing

36 Matthew 5:10
37 Matthew 5:11-12

so and mockingly asking if he would stand up for Jesus.

On a good note, he left the office for a break and when he came back some of his colleagues told him they were on his side and were playing gospel music to upset the coworker who originally made the fuss. My friend, desiring to be the peacemaker told them there weren't any sides and went back to work.

The truth is, persecution is simply a clash between two value systems: The values of this world—money, power, self-interest, and so much more, and the values of God—love, compassion, kindness, and selflessness, to name only a few. Not everyone wants to persecute you. But there will be times when you may be made fun of or may be laughed at for your faith. If or when persecution happens in your life, no matter what form it takes, these attitudes are instrumental in helping you to withstand it.

Note that the blessing for this last attitude is in the present tense, "for theirs *is* the kingdom of heaven." This is because followers of Christ can and do share in the kingdom by living out the words of Jesus.[38] In Scripture, the kingdom of heaven and the kingdom of God are synonymous, one in the same. Heaven is not just a place we go after we die, it is actually present in our lives right now as we live a life with Christ.

As we have journeyed through the Beatitudes we have come full circle. We started with, "Blessed are the poor in spirit, for theirs is the kingdom of heaven."[39] And ended with, "Blessed are those who are persecuted because of righteousness, for theirs is the kingdom of heaven."[40]

Each Beatitude Builds on Itself: Let's look at what has happened in our attitudes thus far that might impact how others treat you and will impact your resilience to persecution:

As you trust fully in God (poor in spirit), mourn the sin in the life of those who are wronging you (mourning), and humbly accept that others might not understand your strength in faith (meekness), you will seek to do what is right (hungering for righteousness) in showing mercy (being merciful) to those who attack you. The pureness of *your* heart (pure in heart) will be seen by others as you seek to make peace (peacemaker) in these situations. You will find comfort in your persecution (blessed are those who are persecuted) hoping that others might get a glimpse of and desire to enter God's kingdom.

---

38 Luke 17:20-21
39 Matthew 5:3
40 Matthew 5:10

A Last Look at the Beatilizer

The kingdom starts as we live a life in Christ and extends into eternity after we die. Not everything in the kingdom here on earth is perfect, but one day it will be when Christ comes again. However, when we face troubles, struggles, and pain on the journey we are on, we are not alone. We have Jesus and his Holy Spirit beside us to guide us every step of the way.

Let's look closer at using the Beatilizer as a tool in your toolbox. First, look at each of these attitudes and sum up where you currently are. Be honest with yourself:

- Is it easy for me to trust God in my life or is he my last resort?
- Do I see the sin in my life and do I grieve that sin? Does seeing the depth of the suffering in the world start to break my heart?
- Do I feel the need to be defensive, in control of those around me, or always right? Do I feel above or better than others?
- When faced with a dilemma, is my first reaction to solve it, or to pray asking for God's guidance? Do I look into God's word to help me solve problems? Do I hunger and thirst to do what is morally and ethically right?
- Do I extend forgiveness, grace, compassion, and empathy to others?
- Do I not only feel sympathy for someone's situation, do I also have an active desire to help their situation?
- Do I consider myself inwardly clean as well as outwardly clean? Am I authentic or do I often hide my true self? Has my vision changed? Do I see people more as God sees people, with loving kindness?
- Am I at peace with myself? Do I seek peace and reconciliation with others?
- When faced with criticism for doing what is right, in living an ethical and moral life following Jesus, does that change me and do I humbly stand strong in my conviction and withstand the persecution? Do I look to Jesus for strength and comfort in these situations?

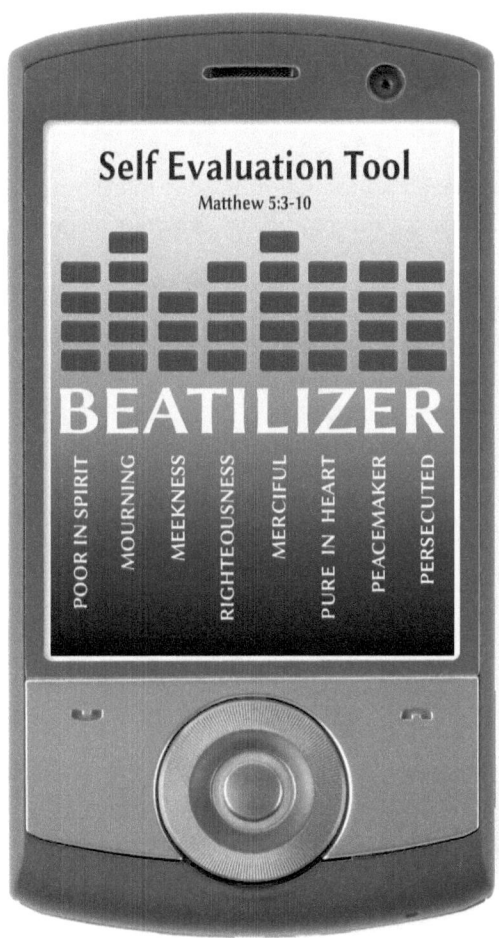

At this point, you might be saying, "Darn (to be honest, I actually said, damn, but for this book I will say darn), I have a lot to work on!"

That's okay my friend! It was the same for me! The important thing is this: If I am now walking with Jesus on this journey, am I willing to listen and apply his wisdom? Am I willing to humble myself to wrestle with answers rather than assume that my solution is best or right?

I recommend looking at the Beatilizer from time to time and review the questions, asking yourself about your attitudes. You will find that as you are honestly seeking his presence, his wisdom, and wrestling with applying it to your life, you will become stronger.

In time your Beatilizer channels may all hover around the half way to three-quarter mark. Rarely will one of the Beatitudes fully top out for long. That's okay. Just keep applying and relying on God to give you strength for the next mile.

Now that we have set a foundation for our journey and have established the right attitudes for continuing on, we can start to look farther ahead on the path.

5
Develop Your Plan

"I Will Be with You"

—God

For I know the plans I have for you, declares the Lord, plans to prosper you and not to harm you, plans to give you hope and a future.

—Jeremiah 29:11

Knowing where we are going is always good. When I was living in Daytona Beach in the early 1980's, I knew I needed help. I cried out to God more times than I can count alone at night, "God, why can't I get things straight in my life? Why is everything so hard? I need your help." I prayed this over and over again knowing I had tried everything on my own and it simply wasn't working. In the Exodus story we are told the people "groaned in their slavery and cried out."[41] That is exactly what it was like with me!

That time in my life taught me that God wants us to understand, not *just* to obey. Don't get me wrong, obedience is important, but I believe understanding why we obey God's wisdom and wanting to do so from the heart is one of the ultimate blessings we can give God. When we pray and ask God for strength to obey his wisdom, he will hear our prayers.

Discerning God's Answers to Our Prayers

Concerning prayer, as I mentioned before, it seems it can be easy to think God is like this cosmic vending machine that pops out a can of soda every time we throw in a dollar. Could he pop out the answer we ask for immediately? Yes. Sometimes he even does. But more often than not, he provides discernment and guidance so we can actively participate in our needs. My friend, Joseph Thompson puts it best this way, "Prayer alone doesn't prevent plane crashes, competent systems and responsibility do. Prayer is not a substitute for the use of common sense, it is a complement."[42]

A friend once emailed me concerning her son who had been caught in a web of addiction for over 15 years. She asked, "I am trying hard not to give up on prayer right now, but sometimes I feel like it's not worth it. What about 'knock and the door shall be opened' and 'ask anything in my name and it shall be given?'"[43]

My answer to her was that God was indeed answering her prayer, just not in the way she expected. Over the years, and even at the time she wrote me, God had crossed the path of this young man in sometimes miraculous ways, with people who wanted to help and who provided him help. This was God answering her prayers. But alas, his decisions and poor choices kept rearing their ugly heads. Prayer is important. Discerning God's answers

---

41 Exodus 2:23
42 Joseph Thompson, *Imagine Say: What if God really Counted on You* (Lake Mary, FL: Primal Church.TV, 2012)
43 Matthew 7:7

to our prayers is just as important. God provides wisdom and answers. He knows that when we participate in the answer, we learn and can be changed in deeper ways than we would be if he just granted our every wish.[44]

> *GUIDING PRINCIPLE: Pray Without Ceasing*
>
> Every journey we encounter, indeed before, during, and after the journey, we should be talking to our guide, Jesus. Communication is important. In 1 Thessalonians 5:16-18, Paul tells us to stay in *constant* communication with God—to pray without ceasing. (See more on this in Appendix 2: Praying Without Ceasing.)

God also heard the cries and prayers of the Hebrew people who were in bondage in Egypt.[45] The answers to their prayer also required action and sacrifice on their part. God defined the route of the Israelites in the Exodus narrative:

> I have indeed seen the misery of my people in Egypt. I have heard them crying out because of their slave drivers, and I am concerned about their suffering. So I have come down to rescue them from the hand of the Egyptians and to bring them up out of that land into a good and spacious land, a land flowing with milk and honey. (Exodus 3:7-8)

Planning the Route

When you go to a mapping website and plan a route from one destination to another, you are almost always given more than one route. Usually, you are given a choice between the fastest, the shortest, and something in-between. Each route has its own set of unique characteristics: toll roads, highways, scenery, traffic levels, and on and on.

If I were wanting to take a trip to the other side of the country, I wouldn't say, "I'm going on a long trip to California, I think I'll just take off and try to figure out how to get there as I go along. Let's see, California is west of me, I guess I will just start driving west and see what happens."

---

44 1 Thessalonians 5:16-18
45 Exodus 2:24-25

DEVELOP YOUR PLAN

The journeys in our lives are much the same way. We can haphazardly just take off in the general direction, or we can plan a route so we will have a good idea of what to expect, avoid trouble spots, and safely get to our destination.

Are you embarking on an exodus out of a bad place? Maybe you need a recovery program or a half-way house. Where will the first leg of your journey be? And after that, where is the second leg of your journey going to take you? Will you go back into the lion's den (the same place that led to your exodus)? What is your destination on this journey?

For me, my destination was to free myself from my dependence on mind altering substances. The first leg of my journey was to get my body clean enough to pass a physical, so I could get back in the military. The second leg of the journey was actually getting back in. I signed up for and then was offered overseas duty. I wanted to move away from where I was living and the toxic life I had been leading so I could focus on staying clean. The third leg was to put enough time (in a safe place) between me and my addiction to be able to resist the temptation of turning back to drugs.

Maybe you are on an altruistic journey toward something bigger than yourself. Let's say you want to become a police officer. The first leg might be to join the Police Explorer program in high school. The second might be to get into the police academy. There are other routes depending on your age and calling. Ask God to help show you the path and the steps to take, then get to work.

Are you on a journey out of the status quo? Maybe the first leg of your journey is finding a church where you can meet new friends or join a small group at your current church. Maybe the second leg of your journey is to get involved and to serve. As always, ask God to help you figure out the path.

Think about the journey you are on and envision the promised land. What will it take to get there? Here are some practical steps for you to consider as you prepare:

Pray! This is always the first step. Ask God to help you find a route, to cross your path with earthly helpers and to give you the strength to take the first steps. Ask God to help you understand your journey and to find people to help you along the way. Ask for strength and discernment.

Next, pray more! Find your next layer of help. Find a trusted friend or family member. Maybe you already know someone. Ask their counsel. You are looking for someone who will be encouraging but honest; for someone who will think in your best interest. It doesn't hurt to have a few people like this around you. Pastors are often very good at this. I often tell people, "Can I be Frank? I will be Pastor Jan later." Go look for Frank. Research the steps you need to get to where you are going. You have now planned the first legs of your journey. If you are just on this journey called life and don't have any specific places you can see you need to go, though you know something is needed, it's a good idea to ask God what to do next. It's always good to have some direction in life for your travels.

Identifying Trouble Spots

Each unique journey has unique trouble spots. When we are aware of what to expect, we are better able to overcome them as obstacles, or even better yet, avoid some if possible. God helped Moses see some trouble spots for the Israelites:

> When Pharaoh let the people go, God did not lead them on the road through the Philistine country, though that was shorter. For God said, "If they face war, they might change their minds and return to Egypt." God led the people around by the desert road toward the Red Sea. The Israelites went up out of Egypt ready for battle. (Exodus 13:17-18)

On the journey out of their hostile environment, the Israelites faced many obstacles. On your journey, you undoubtedly will too. With Jesus as your journey companion, you will find that often these obstacles are overcome in very spiritual ways.

In my own journey from addiction, when God answered my prayers and gave me a way to put drugs behind me, I made the decision to obey. I had tried and failed, tried and failed for years. In fact, look at how my decisions "helped" me. I moved from Melbourne to Daytona Beach which is one of the party capitals of Florida. My hope was that I would be able to manage my addiction more effectively away from all my drug using friends. The truth was, I stayed high almost 24/7 with new drug using friends! I only managed to live in my own self-destruction.

Once I decided to obey his wisdom and surrender to him, God gave me a miracle. He gave me the strength to do in six months what I had been trying to do for six years—get clean.

I remember getting up in the morning, leaving my rented room in Daytona Beach, and running the trails in the woods so I could prepare myself physically for my return to military service. I was able to go into the recruiter's office and schedule a physical knowing I was clean. First obstacle down. I credit God—indeed Jesus—with giving me the strength to knock down this obstacle. He was my guide, both day and night.[46]

> *GUIDING PRINCIPLE: Give Credit to God*
> Look for the blessing and give credit where credit is due. Don't take the credit yourself; give it to the one who truly gave you the strength to overcome. When Jesus is your guide, he will lead, you just need to follow.

The other miracle, in my mind, is that even my friends who used drugs with me, supported my decision to get clean rather than cajole me into staying in that destructive party world. They even stopped using in front of me.

If you are embarking on a journey out of a bad place believe me, there will be many, many trouble spots. There will be trouble spots no matter what kind of journey you are on. They are unavoidable. So, expect them, but also resolve to overcome them, and pray. I have found that most of these trouble spots are overcome with the combination of prayer and listening and looking for God's answers.

Making the Decision to Go

The hardest part to starting a journey is very often, making the decision to go. That decision requires change and stepping away from what is familiar into an unknown future.

Making the decision to go if you are on a journey out of a bad place.

I see this so often as a pastor: Abused women staying with their man because they hope he will get better. People caught up in addiction also often feel they will somehow be able to learn to manage their addiction and get better. Yet, they persist in their bondage because they can't make the decision to leave it. The doors seem closed, but often they are open and waiting to be walked through, if one is willing to make the decision to do so.

46 Exodus 13:21

I had a friend who was homeless and an alcoholic. God crossed our paths in a rather remarkable way and I told him what I have told so many caught in addiction, "If you ever want to get clean, let me know. I can help you get into recovery and find a path out."

He told me that he already had been in recovery—for a whole month. I laughed to myself. That wasn't recovery. There is no possible way that in one month anyone can put the physical and mental addiction to substances behind them. Around the same time, a woman who had confessed addiction was ruining her life told me the very same thing. I laughed to myself again, because it simply couldn't be true.

I'm happy to say, that after many, many months of my friend saying he needed change and to start recovery but resisting that change at the same time—after many months of praying, he finally decided to go to rehab. At the time of this writing he is voluntarily in a men's facility, no longer living in a tent, and making great progress. The key is, he made the decision to go.

The woman I mentioned, who was offered the same opportunity, as of this writing, to my knowledge, is stuck in the same old circle of wanting to make the decision to go, but just not doing it. What keeps someone from making the decision that will change their life? I believe there are a few things going on under the surface.

Making the decision to go requires admitting a decision needs to be made. Many people live in total denial of their circumstance or simply accept it as their lot in life. Moses encountered this with the enslaved Israelites, they simply didn't want to listen.[47]

My homeless friend I mentioned above had a camp mate out in the woods who, in many ways, was worse off than him. After my friend started rehab I went out to their camp to get some of his belongings. There was his camp mate, drunk as usual. He heard me walk into camp and crawled out from under a makeshift tarp tent that was flat on the ground, beaten down from the rain the night before. I told him that our mutual friend had entered a recovery program. He agreed our friend needed the recovery. The woods were not for him. But this man himself? Hey, he could stop drinking on a dime. He didn't need alcohol. Besides, he liked "camping." I gave him my card in case he ever changed his mind.

---

47 God told Moses to tell the Israelites he would bring them out of bondage and free them from their slavery. Exodus 6:9: "Moses reported this to the Israelites, but they did not listen to him because of their discouragement and harsh labor."

Asking for Assistance

While we've already mentioned seeking wise counsel, let's take a deeper look at this important element:

I firmly believe God puts people in our path to help us along the way. We can tell he put them there because they have our best interest at heart, will be encouraging, honest (letting you know when you are making a bad decision), and above all else, will always point you God's way rather than their own, and will never suggest you take illegal or immoral shortcuts.

Always be on the lookout for Satan and his crew. I hesitate to share this story, but it is a pretty good example. A few years back, I was ministering to a prostitute who was really trying to get her life right. She was doing a pretty good job of it. Around this time, I had been teaching her about prayer.

One day she called and with exasperation in her voice said, "Pastor Jan, I prayed this morning and asked God for five dollars. That's all I need to get some food. I walked down to the library in Sanford and on the way a man stopped me and offered me $5 to… [he wanted to buy her services for a few minutes]. Was that God answering my prayer?"

"Heaven's no girl!" I answered, "I hope you didn't take it! (She hadn't.) That was the devil trying to tempt you back!"

> *GUIDING PRINCIPLE: Recognize the Opposing Forces*
>
> Whenever we make a decision to follow God, there are spiritual forces (Satan and his minions) that will seek to slow you down and wear you out, all in hopes of you deciding to turn back. Prayer and perseverance are your best weapons. Know these forces can't stop you, but they will try to make you turn back on your own. (See more on this in Appendix 3: Recognizing the Opposing Forces.) You have items of defense at your disposal.

Interestingly enough, my friend would often hide cash in the bushes around Sanford so her crack head husband wouldn't be able to take it from her. Being drunk, she would often forget where she stashed her money, but that was better than him taking it from her.

She called me the next day and told me she had found five dollars she had hidden in the bushes probably days before. You see, she resisted doing the wrong thing and, in the end, God answered her prayer.

I had another friend that had gotten out of prison after a 14-year stint. He sought wise counsel in a childhood friend, a very godly woman who was helping him discern the right things to do to stay out of trouble. He was also seeing a therapist who was a counselor I had known for almost a decade. His friend asked me to speak with him when she found out I also knew his counselor. His friend introduced us, and we hit it off right away. Early on he confided in me that it was hard sometimes for him to feel God's presence. I told him he was doing the right thing and to keep listening to God.

Do you see how no one could have orchestrated these people in his life or managed this any better? God had put all these players in place to help this man. God gave him the strength to ask for and accept assistance rather than just trying to get on with life after incarceration. God was in control of the situation and was leading my friend. He continues to do well and has overcome much of his troubled past.

We cannot make a journey like this on our own. We might eventually get somewhere near our destination, but with God's assistance (and through his provision of wise council) we will get there in much better shape. Ask God to cross your path with people who will assist you on your journey and to discern when they are godly people. Like I told my friend that prayed for some food money, "Don't take five dollars from just anybody!"

Breaking Down the Walls

When I was in the Army my drill sergeant used to pound into us that if we faced a wall in our path, we had better go over it, under it, around it or through it. Above all else, we better not let it stop us. Walls keep us from going where we need to go. Walls also keep us trapped inside. What walls are keeping you from going where you need to go?

Making the decision to go if you are on a journey out of a bad place.

If you are contemplating a journey out of a bad place in life, practical things like jobs and possessions are often reasons that keep us from starting our journeys. I have often seen people lose these things even if they decide not to embark on their journey out of a bad place. Let's take a closer look at some reasons that can keep us from making the decision to go, despite being in a bad place:

Friends, relatives, and our relationships, are often one of the first reasons

I hear people tell me as to why they don't go. Even in this, there are many things that just don't really make sense. There are basically three camps of friends and relatives. First, there are those who truly want us to succeed in life, but we have a hard time leaving them, even when they would support and stand beside us if we sought the help we needed. In the second camp are those friends and relatives that want us to stay right where we are and tell us we'll never make it, it's futile, we don't need help, etc. Lastly, in the third camp, there are the ones enabling our enslavement, our party friends and relatives, our abusers. These people don't want us to go most of all.

Moses had this third camp kind of problem in Exodus. Pharaoh and his officials realized that letting the Israelites go would mean they were losing their slaves.[48] I implore you, run from these people! They only have their own interest at heart.

The truth is those who truly love us for our own good and not theirs will stand by us and help us get better. Those who don't, well, we should run from them anyway. Unfortunately, they are toxic to our lives. Don't let these relationships keep you back.

There are other reasons that might keep us from making a decision to seek the help we need. We might feel guilty because we should have never come to this place in life at all. Did you get that, feeling guilty because you never should have let yourself get in this bad place is actually keeping you from getting out. Sure, it doesn't make sense on paper, yet it's often a powerful reality we have to face.

Fear of the unknown also keeps us from departing. Here is what I say on this: It's painful where you are, and it will be painful moving ahead. There is nothing you can do to avoid it either way. Don't let the fear of the unknown outweigh the reality of the pain you are already in. What is ahead will be better.

> *GUIDING PRINCIPLE: Choose Your Pain*
>
> It is painful getting out of a bad situation but staying in one only gets worse and leads to more pain. If you are in a bad place it rarely (if ever) gets better. While it's painful taking the steps to get out, they will always lead to less pain. Which is the better pain to choose? Choose the pain that gets better not worse. Why stay sick on purpose?

---

48 Exodus 14:5

Society can be a reason we use to prevent ourselves from leaving a bad place in order to restore our life and reach the promised land. We care what society will think: *I'm a failure. I can't keep it together.* We allow society to pressure us. Unfortunately, many times we have reached a level of "functioning" in our bad situation. Meaning that often the pain, addiction, or abuse is behind closed doors and rarely, if ever, gets out in the open. Don't let this stop you from starting out on your journey. You will be so much more useful to society when you are made whole. Go!

Pride is another thing that keeps us from embarking on an exodus to wholeness. You know what people say the Bible tells us about pride, right? It comes before the fall.[49] Don't let yourself fall, start moving forward in life and leave the pride that pins you down behind.

Shame often keeps us from starting our journey. We may feel shame because we can't control ourselves, or because we let ourselves get in this position in the first place. In a situation of coming out of abuse, we may feel shame because we simply cannot be good enough to please our partner. We can become a slave to shame by not loving ourselves enough to go.

Lastly, there are often practical things like jobs and possessions that we use as reasons to keep us from starting our journey. I have often seen people lose their jobs and possessions even if they decide not to embark on their journey out of a bad place. We can only function so long before the house of cards begins to fall. We can get our jobs and possessions back if we lose them by taking the journey out of our bad place. But we gain nothing if we stay addicted and in pain.

Relationships, guilt, fear, society, pride, shame, jobs and possessions can keep us from starting our journey. Don't let them have the final say. Make the decision, ask God to help you, and develop a plan.

Making the decision to go if you are on a journey into a good place.

What if your journey is on the other side of the spectrum and not so much about leaving a bad place but about going to a better one?

In 2003 I felt called to be a pastor. I felt like God had given me a desire

---

49 I think it is a little humorous that everyone thinks the Bible says pride comes before the fall! (Usually heard in a loud, thunderous voice like it is coming directly from God). While I think there is much wisdom in the fact that pride comes before the fall, the Bible doesn't actually say that. What the Bible actually says is this: "Pride goes before destruction, a haughty spirit before a fall" (Proverbs 16:18). So, even more so: Don't let your pride destroy you. Go!

to serve him and others in a way that was much bigger than myself. Just like Moses and all his reasons, I fought it and debated my case to God.

God told Moses: "So now, go. I am sending you to Pharaoh to bring my people the Israelites out of Egypt." But Moses said to God, "Who am I that I should go to Pharaoh and bring the Israelites out of Egypt?"[50]

I told God: "Lord, who am I to be a pastor? I messed that up many years ago with my drug addiction."

God told both of us: "I will be with you."[51]

Moses had another argument: "What if they do not believe me or listen to me and say, 'The LORD did not appear to you'?"[52]

I also had another argument: "Lord, I don't have the education. Who will accept that I can become a pastor?"

God told Moses he would take care of it and told him the staff in his hand, as well as some simple water, through miracles, would demonstrate Moses had indeed received his guidance and the people would believe and listen.[53]

God told me: Enter my classroom and get ready for some tough lessons. I will lead you and show you what you need to know.

Moses had yet another argument: "Pardon your servant, Lord. I have never been eloquent, neither in the past nor since you have spoken to your servant. I am slow of speech and tongue."[54]

I had yet another argument: I have never been a speaker or much of a teacher.

At this point, I think God was getting perturbed: He told Moses, "Who gave human beings their mouths? Who makes them deaf or mute? Who gives them sight or makes them blind? Is it not I, the LORD? Now go; I will help you speak and will teach you what to say."[55]

And, God basically said the same thing to me!

Still, Moses argued one more time and said, "Pardon your servant, Lord. Please send someone else."[56]

Then God got pretty mad and told Moses his brother Aaron would do the talking.

---

50 Exodus 3:10-11
51 Exodus 3:12
52 Exodus 4:1
53 Exodus 4:2-9
54 Exodus 4:10
55 Exodus 4:11
56 Exodus 4:13

God pretty much told me: Tough luck, I would have to do my own talking!

I had other concerns too. At the time I was working in corporate America making a pretty penny. I knew if I followed his calling I would earn much less. His answer was to tell me to prepare to make less. So, I started doing that. I started paying off bills (God placed Financial Peace University in my life just at the right time. [57]) Eventually my wife and I got to a place financially that we didn't need the larger amount of money I was making. Funny though, our basic standard of living never changed. How does God do this stuff?

As you can see, and may have already experienced, God rarely ask us to take the easy road. It can be hard and scary to face these decisions. The good news is that the road he asks you to take will always, always help you grow.

> **GUIDING PRINCIPLE:** *The Box Principle*
>
> God often asks us to step outside our box. We often go kicking and screaming, "Now, where do you want me to go? Here are all my reasons why I can't Lord!" But when we are obedient to God—we grow in ways we would never imagine. Step out of your box and let Jesus lead the way. I promise, he won't let you get lost.

Identifying Possible Problems and Solutions

I have a young friend who just turned 20. He has had a tough life, and for years has said he wants to go into the Navy. As his pastor and friend, I know the Navy would give my young friend opportunities and help instill discipline that up until now, has not been there.

After repeatedly making the decision to go and repeatedly having things not working out in life by doing it his own way, I talked him into trying things another way—God's way.

I accompanied him to the Navy recruiter's office. He was full of confidence and ready to go. The recruiter informed him he needed 15 credit hours of college since he only had a GED. I could see my young friend's heart dropping as he heard this.

---

57 Financial Peace University is a 13-week program on learning to use God's wisdom in application to your finances. It changed my life and can change yours. www.daveramsey.com

DEVELOP YOUR PLAN

This was another obstacle, but I didn't want this to stop him. So we prayed. We asked God to show him the way. He was ready to give up but instead, we started identifying possible problems and solutions.

Next, we went to the local college and talked to them about what he needed to do to get those 15 credit hours. Everything was looking good. Then a small paperwork snafu came up. Again, he was defeated.

"No, no, no!" I said. "Let's pray!" We did.

A short time later my young friend called telling me that he was going for it. He was signing up for classes and on the way to college to get those 15 credits.

We simply cannot let obstacles stop us. We must search for ways to overcome them. Start by praying and give God the glory when the answer is presented. When presented with an obstacle, there is almost always a way to overcome it. Find the way. Jesus says, "Seek and you will find."[58] He knows life better than we know life, He's the author of it.

Closing the Loops (Not Burning Bridges)

When we are embarking on a journey, we are leaving one place to go to another—leaving something behind. But we don't leave everything behind and we don't want to destroy everything either. Ultimately, if we want to travel on the spiritual strength of God, we must seek and give forgiveness, always exhibit kindness, be fair, honest, moral, and ethical.

Why do I even mention this again, "Duh, isn't this what this book is about?" Yes it is, however, our human inclination is often to justify our decisions and not always in healthy ways. We want to put blame on people, places, and things to give strength to the decisions we are making.

On my journey of fulfilling my call to become a pastor, I was also on a journey out of a place I was not entirely happy in. I was a purchaser and financial administrator for three companies owned by one person. I often felt I was asked to compromise my ethics in the commission of my duties. There were times I feared losing my job for my decisions to be honest and fair with customers and suppliers. From my boss's perspective, it was just business, yet from mine, I needed to be true to myself in Christ. I could have easily left these companies hanging and hurting by leaving. However, that also would not have been ethical in my mind. So, here is what I did: I worked out with my new employer (the church) to offer my old employer four weeks' notice

58 Matthew 7:7-8

rather than the standard two and I also offered them three months paid consulting to train my replacement. During those three months I worked two jobs, but it was the right thing to do.

Lastly, there are those who are enablers: party friends and people who are not good for you because they tempt you to stay in your bad place. You should also forgive them in your heart, but not necessarily burn the bridge of your relationship (unless it is truly toxic), just step away kindly, and have nothing to do with them until you are able to resist their peer pressure to reenter the world you are leaving. There may and probably will come a time that you are strong enough to stand on your own in their presence and not be tempted to do the wrong things. But that time is reserved for the future after you have gained much strength on your journey.

Be very careful about burning bridges! Be careful with justifying yourself and the decisions you want to make. Instead of throwing out blame, even when due, we should kindly step away, do everything in our power to forgive, and leave. We don't need to leave a path of destruction on our way to the promised land. What is important about not burning bridges (no matter what the journey) is that in the future, healthy relationships can be restored.

"I Will Be with You"

There are a million reasons not to embark on a journey. Here is the main point to be made: Pray, talk with God, consult with him, and listen for his guidance. If you feel you need to embark, do it! Trust in him and know that he will be with you each step of the way. Remember, God told Moses, "I will be with you."[59]

---

59 Exodus 3:12

6
The Hardest Part is Leaving

"You have to let go at some point in order to move forward."

—C.S. Lewis

Let your eyes look straight ahead;
fix your gaze directly before you.
Give careful thought to the paths for your feet
and be steadfast in all your ways.

— Proverbs 4:25-26

Saying, "so long" or "good bye" is always tough. Every time I step into the unknown, either on a journey out of a bad place or even on a journey into a good place, there is a certain fear of the unknown that grips me. My faith in God always overtakes that fear and carries me through. But, for my faith in God to carry me through the fear, I still must experience the fear.

As part of my job as a pastor, I am allowed a sabbatical of thirty days every seven years. I am enjoying that sabbatical as I write these words. I have spent the better half of the last eight months in preparation of this month alone with God. It was an exhilarating experience preparing for this time in the mountains of Tennessee. Yet, as I got within weeks of leaving, there was still a fear of the unknown, a fear for me of what thirty days alone with God, away from my normal routine and daily life would be like.

In the journey from bondage, especially from a bad place, it is always a quandary for me to understand why we don't just let go and let God take control. When I see a woman caught in an abusive relationship, I ask myself, *Why don't you just develop a plan and leave?* When I see someone caught up in addiction, especially once they recognize it is ruining their life, I ask myself, *Why don't you just leave?*

The spiritual battle that Moses had with Pharaoh is so similar to the battles we face within ourselves. When I left my addiction behind, like Moses, I had to battle with my own pharaoh, that self-doubting side of myself which refused to let me go. This is what it is like for so many people when it comes time to making the decision to leave their current circumstances and to finally do it.

We battle with ourselves, almost to the death (sadly sometimes literally), to do what we know is right. Look closely at the following paragraphs; there are parallels between the battle Moses faced in setting the Hebrew people free and the battle we face to set ourselves free.

I see Moses as us and Pharaoh as that voice of fear, doubt, and pride that resides in us. God's voice is deep inside us pushing to do the right thing. All the while he knows that if we give in to our own pharaoh, that self-doubting voice, we will never leave our bondage. In some ways I see Moses' brother, Aaron, who God said would be the spokesman between Moses and Pharaoh, as the Holy Spirit, the helper on our journey:

Exodus 6:28-30 says:

> Now when the LORD spoke to Moses in Egypt, he said to him, "I am the LORD. Tell Pharaoh king of Egypt everything I tell you." But Moses said to the LORD, "Since I speak with faltering lips, why would Pharaoh listen to me?"

In our hearts we hear: Now when God's voice inside spoke to me, he said to me, 'I am the LORD.' Tell that self-doubting voice inside everything I tell you. But I said to the LORD, Since I speak with faltering lips, why would that self-doubting voice listen to me?

Exodus 7:1-5 says:

> Then the LORD said to Moses, "See, I have made you like God to Pharaoh, and your brother Aaron will be your prophet. You are to say everything I command you, and your brother Aaron is to tell Pharaoh to let the Israelites go out of his country. But I will harden Pharaoh's heart, and though I multiply my signs and wonders in Egypt, he will not listen to you. Then I will lay my hand on Egypt and with mighty acts of judgment I will bring out my divisions, my people the Israelites. And the Egyptians will know that I am the LORD when I stretch out my hand against Egypt and bring the Israelites out of it."

In our hearts we hear: Then God's voice said to me, See, I have made you like the master to that self-doubting voice inside you, and your helper the Holy Spirit will be your prophet. You are to say everything I command you, and the Holy Spirit will tell that self-doubting voice inside to let yourself go out of this bondage you are in. But I will harden that self-doubting voice inside your heart, and though I multiply my signs and wonders in your life and your heart, he will not listen to you. Then I will lay my hand on your heart and with mighty acts of judgment I will bring out my divisions, that part of you in bondage. And those around you will know that I am the LORD when I stretch out my hand against your bondage and bring you out of it.

Does this sound familiar? Does a battle rage inside, trying to keep you from making the decision to go and to finally embark on the journey out of your bondage? By the way, we are also in bondage if we are having a hard time leaving our status quo, or even moving into a good place in life. We can hear God's voice inside saying, "It's time to go, it's time to get out of this!" Yet that self-doubting voice inside keeps holding us back.

In the Exodus story there is a great spiritual battle that transpires through a series of plagues on Egypt which should, by any stretch of the heart, have convinced Pharaoh to let God's people go. In each of these ten plagues, Pharaoh comes closer and closer to letting them go, and in many instances says, "Ok, you can go!" but then reneges on his promise and keeps them in bondage.

It is much the same for us. Something happens in our life that should convince us to embark on the journey out and we come so close to doing it saying, "Alright already, I'm going!" But the fear of the unknown sneaks up on us and we turn around saying, "Nope! I'm staying where I am!"

Additionally, each of these ten plagues got worse until the last one culminated in death. In the case of Pharaoh, it was the death of the first born which included his own first-born son. Sadly, I also see this at times in people's lives today. It takes a near death experience, a terrible beating, or an overdose for example, to finally take steps to leave the bondage.

After Pharaoh finally relented and allowed God's people to leave, he again changed his mind and attempted to bring them back into bondage. Once we start to get free and clear of the bondage that is killing us both physically and spiritually, that self-doubting voice seeks to convince us to stay. We must always drown out that self-doubting voice with God's voice and through his Holy Spirit continue our journey out of bondage.

Even when our journey is into a good place, there is often a self-doubting voice inside doing battle to keep us from making that change, trying to prevent us from saying goodbye, so we can't say hello to a new journey in life.

The hardest part is always leaving. Even if we want change, our familiar surroundings give us a sense of security. We know what to expect where we are, but if we leave, we don't exactly know what lies ahead. It takes faith to leave. Trust in Jesus and trust in his wisdom. Recognize that God will give you refuge and strength in times of trouble and there is nothing to fear.[60] Knowing the fear of leaving where you are is tough and preparing for it is better than simply allowing your fear to hold you back. In the end acknowledging the fear might actually make it easier for you to leave.

As I mentioned earlier, I wrote most of this book while on a sabbatical

---

60 Psalm 46:1-3

high on Roan Mountain in Tennessee. As I prepared to go on this thirty-day sabbatical and faced my own fear of the unknown (being away from my family and routine) I recognized that self-doubting voice inside of me. But I also heard God's strong voice too. His voice made it easier to say, "Be back soon!"

The Path Isn't Always Smooth

As we journey through life we want to take the path that is easiest to travel. Yet, even these paths can be fraught with challenges. If we expect challenges and struggles, they are easier to overcome, and we can learn each step of the way. However, when we face hurdles on our own, applying our worldly wisdom, we are often faced with even more challenges because of the decisions we were making. But when Jesus is our guide, challenges are easier to navigate because we apply his wisdom as we face them. Don't expect a smooth path; expect and know Jesus will help you navigate through obstacles as you travel with him.

> *GUIDING PRINCIPLE: Everything in Between is Messy*
>
> Most of us are born into this world loved. For many, early childhood was grand. We were loved by God with an undeniable love that even if we didn't realize it, strengthened us and moved us forward. But, at some point most of us began to engage life on our own terms and stray from that wisdom and love. There is a beautiful beginning to a life born into this world. For those of us who have accepted the call of Jesus, the ending of our earthly life to an eternity with God the Father is a beautiful ending. But, sandwiched between this beautiful beginning and beautiful ending is a bunch of messiness. If we recognize life is messy, and we trust and rely on God for our strength to face each period of messiness, our journey becomes smoother because of the lessons learned.

Walk, Don't Run

There is a bit of Christian worldly wisdom I do not resonate with. Have you ever heard someone say, "Be careful, never pray for patience, because then God will send you trials to teach you patience?" This is backward logic.

THE HARDEST PART IS LEAVING

Trials are coming regardless of how you pray.

I think it's safe to say we all want patience but it's just so hard to actually be patient. Impatience often makes us vulnerable because there is a sense of desperation. We live in an instant world, we want instant gratification. When we are impatient we often make rash decisions rather than informed ones. This is the weakness of impatience. There is a strength in being patient although it is hard to learn patience because it takes, well, patience.

In Exodus, Moses was following God's plan. Exodus 13:17-18 says, "When Pharaoh let the people go, God did not lead them on the road through the Philistine country, though that was shorter. For God said, 'If they face war, they might change their minds and return to Egypt.' So God led the people around by the desert road toward the Red Sea."

If we trust Jesus and allow him to guide us, the journey may not be the fastest route, but I can assure you, it will be the best one.

My mentor and pastor, Phil, often tells me, "Life is a marathon, it's not a race!" We need to pace ourselves and not sprint. We need to have patience and pace ourselves to reach the finish line and not burn out. In this hustle bustle world, we want everything immediately. We can often have things faster if we push the issue, but this often will leave us vulnerable and winded, sometimes even wounded. Recognize your journey is a marathon, not a race. Pacing yourself, along with God at your side, is the healthiest way to go.

In my own altruistic journey of being called to be a pastor, there were five years between the time I recognized the call in 2003 to when I was actually ordained in 2008. As I look back, I can see now that it was all in God's timing. I was not ready to be ordained as a pastor in 2003 even though I wanted to be. I spent those years allowing God to guide me, shape me, and teach me so when the time did come, I was truly ready.

Here is an interesting tidbit, the apostle Paul was called by Jesus on the road to Damascus.[61] However, it was three years before Paul even met the Apostles and it would be another fourteen years before Paul actually started his ministry as an apostle.[62]

Everything is in God's timing whether we want it to be or not. We need to welcome and live in his timing, with patience, so we can be properly prepared. Keep praying for patience on your journey. The prophet Isaiah tells us God acts on behalf of those who wait for him.[63] Be patient, Jesus is leading the way.

61 Acts 9:3-6
62 Galatians 1:18-24; 2:1
63 Isaiah6:4

Watch Out for Obstacles

When I was in the Army, we were taught that as we led a platoon on a foot march through unknown territory, we must always be careful to take in our surroundings and be on the lookout for obstacles, traps, and the enemy. This was the best and safest way to get to our intended objective. In the journeys we are talking about here, our objective is our promised land.

I find that as we identify obstacles in our path, as we identify traps and the enemy (Satan), many of these obstacles are overcome in very supernatural ways, meaning, they are overcome as answers to prayer.

When Moses was leading God's people out of bondage, they were immediately faced with a huge obstacle. The Red Sea.[64] Most importantly, Pharaoh (remember he's that little self-doubting voice we talked about earlier) had a change of heart and was again pursuing the Israelites. Pharaoh's army actually caught up with God's people and they were terrified. Listen to their reaction just a short while into their journey and tell me we don't sometimes think this way, especially when we are trying to be in control of our circumstances: "Was it because there were no graves in Egypt that you brought us to the desert to die? What have you done to us by bringing us out of Egypt? Didn't we say to you in Egypt, 'Leave us alone; let us serve the Egyptians'? It would have been better for us to serve the Egyptians than to die in the desert!"[65]

So often, when we are faced with the first seemingly insurmountable obstacle as we journey ahead, we second guess our choices and beat ourselves up. I encourage you not to do this. This is Satan trying to get us to turn back and not follow God. Don't fall for his trap. How did Moses react to that self-doubting voice inside the people? He said, "Do not be afraid. Stand firm and you will see the deliverance the LORD will bring you today."[66]

Here is another small but important detail in the Exodus story. After Moses tells the Israelites not to be afraid, he tells them to sit tight, be quiet, and relax, "The LORD will fight for you; you need only to be still."[67] While this might be what God tells us to do at times, this was not one of them. God had told Moses to move on from where they were, yet Moses, not trusting God, took matters into his own hands. Not surprisingly, God became stern with Moses and said, "Why are you crying out to me? Tell the Israelites to

64 Exodus 13:18
65 Exodus 14:5-12
66 Exodus 14:13
67 Exodus 14:14

move on. Raise your staff and stretch out your hand over the sea to divide the water so that the Israelites can go through the sea on dry ground."[68]

The key point here is don't just sit still, doing nothing, expecting God to save you. He will provide a way, but he also wants you to act. You are part of the solution. The solution may not be as in your face miraculous as parting the Red Sea...although it could be.

> *GUIDING PRINCIPLE : Be Still and Know God is in Control*
>
> Psalm 46 starts with, "God is our refuge and strength, an ever-present help in trouble." Verse 10 says, "Be still and know that I am God". We often feel like we survive by the sweat of our brow, God is telling us to calm our hearts and put our trust in him. **He will still call on us to do the work**, he just wants us to relax and trust in his leading.

Don't Get Lost

A friend of mine once told me that following Jesus was like having an internal GPS. Without our GPS, sometimes we easily get lost. If we use our GPS properly we can get to our destination. But, we must enter the destination, or it can't help us find our way. The lessons from the Exodus story, Beatitudes, and many other tools God gives us to navigate this life successfully won't do any good if we don't apply them to our hearts, our minds, and to our lives. It's time to enter the destination into *your* GPS (God Positioning System) and hit go.

I like to ask people, "Why do you think it took forty years for the Israelites to reach the promised land?"[69] It's because they kept turning away from God and going off the spiritual path. Even though they had seen God's glory in so many ways, they were still arrogant in their attitudes.

God had delivered them out of Egypt through the ten plagues; they miraculously crossed over the Red Sea where they were led by a pillar of fire at night and a cloud of smoke by day. God even miraculously provided

---

68 Exodus 14:15-16
69 Deuteronomy 1:1 tells us it takes only eleven days to go from Horeb (that is the mountain range that includes Mt. Sinai) to Kadesh Barnea. This would have been the second leg of their journey. And it should have only taken eleven days or so—all total, it should have only taken two-to-four months, but instead it took over forty years!

manna for food. But still they grumbled, moaned, and turned to idols. God was with them, showing them his love through all these miracles, and even with all of that, they kept turning away from God—they just wouldn't trust his leading.[70]

There are lessons in this for us. Trusting God saves us from wandering through the desert for forty years when the journey should only take two-to-four months. We are to be content with what we have, trust in his leading, be obedient, grateful, and faithful to him.[71] If we do these things we will have nothing to fear.[72] Had the Israelites done this, it would not have taken them so long to reach the promised land. We need to spend a lot of time in prayer, asking his guidance, praising him, thanking him, and, if we hear redirection is needed, we should respond as soon as that GPS goes off. In other words, anticipate all that you will face on your journey and don't let temptations, dangers, and mirages throw you off course.

Let's look a little closer at potential hurdles we may face across the vast expanse of desert we will navigate through:

Temptations: You will be tempted to return to your old way of thinking. You will be tempted to take shortcuts off the paths set out before you. You will be tempted to see where you came from as an easier place to be than the journey you are on.

This is where the armor of God comes in.[73] Wear your breastplate of righteousness, your helmet of salvation and your belt buckle of truth. You need these tools to help you withstand the onslaught of self-doubt and the appearance of false paths presented by the adversary.

Focus on the first beatitude, "Blessed are the poor in spirit" as you put your trust in God's leading rather than your own or worse, the leading of the great deceiver, Satan.[74] Look at your GPS constantly. Ensure you are traveling the route God put before you, and, if you do go a little off course, let your GPS guide you back immediately.

Dangers: Yes, you will face them. You will face many of the same dangers that you face on the regular journey of life. Dangers like accidents, illness, sickness, irritations, warring people, thorny people, storms, poisoned thoughts and ideas, stress, and times when your reserves are low or completely spent.

---

70 1 Corinthians 10:1-5
71 Hebrews 13:5-6
72 Philippians 4:7
73 See Appendix 4: "The Armor of God: Tools You Need on Your Journey"
74 Matthew 5:3

At times like these, focus on the Beatitudes. Be merciful to others, meek in heart, a peacemaker, hunger and thirst for righteousness, and be humble in persecution. Wear the breastplate of righteousness and carry your sword of the spirit and your shield of faith. Let your feet be fitted with the gospel of peace throughout your journey. You especially need these tools when dealing with thorny people, irritations, and through stressful times.

Mirages: Satan will have you thinking that you didn't need to go so far after all and have already arrived at your destination. He may have you thinking you didn't even need to go on this journey at all, or that it is okay to take a shortcut just this once.

Your belt buckle of truth and shield of faith will come in very handy in these instances as will the helmet of salvation.

When you have a strong foundation in the Beatitudes, and a strong understanding and use of the armor of God, it will help energize you and keep your GPS tracking so you can stay on your course. You will be able to face anything thrown at you, including yourself. You got this!

1
Focusing on the Journey

"Difficult roads often lead to beautiful destinations."

— Zig Ziglar

Trust in the LORD with all your heart
and lean not on your own understanding;
in all your ways submit to him,
and he will make your paths straight.

— Proverbs 3:5-6

At this point on our journey, we have made the decision to go and we have generally mapped out the path we are taking. We have identified major obstacles we might face and have thought about possible solutions. We have mentally prepared ourselves and are adjusting our attitudes. We have our gear. It is time to start moving.

The Fork in the Road

This is where it is so important to check your GPS. Earlier we talked briefly about the journey the Israelites took out of bondage in Egypt and noted that a two-to-four-month journey, as it was supposed to be, took over forty years. What path will you take in the quest for your promised land?

This is the fork in the road. This is where you choose—will you journey on your own path or will you take the path with Jesus as your guide? This is the only shortcut you should consider taking, and really, it's not a shortcut, it's just the best path. Both paths are fraught with obstacles, temptations, and struggles. But choosing the path alongside Jesus will prevent you from wandering unnecessarily as the Israelites did. He will help you overcome. He will be your guide.

You have these great God ordained tools at your disposal. You have these attitudes of heart that will carry you further than any worldly wisdom will carry you. You have the armor of God to protect you, and you have your GPS (God Positioning System), as well as your Beatilizer to help keep you on the right track. Take them with you. Use them at every turn and in every situation as you journey with Jesus toward your promised land.

Don't Miss the Signs

The Israelites had a great pillar of cloud to follow by day and a pillar of fire to give them light at night so they could travel at all times.[75] I have always wondered, with these two miracles leading them through the desert, why didn't God's children immediately and forever trust and obey? The Israelites were faced with miracles at almost every turn, but still, they did not listen or trust God. Let's look at the miracles they saw.

The Israelites witnessed the ten plagues against Egypt and in most cases,

Scripture specifically says they were spared. Finally, after the Passover (the plague of the death of the firstborn), and after 430 years in Egypt, Pharaoh set the Israelites free.[76]

Pharaoh then goes back on his word and his army pursues the fleeing Israelites as they start their journey out of Egypt. As the Israelites come upon the Red Sea, the chariots of Pharaoh are in hot pursuit. But Moses parts the waters, the Israelites rush through, and the water swallows up the advancing army of Pharaoh behind them.[77]

Three days later, the Israelites are without water, the only body of water they come across is bitter, and they groan and complain. I kind of understand why they would complain only having bitter water. At this point however, after having seen so many miracles in their lives, I'm surprised the Israelites still didn't trust God would provide for them. Yet, despite this, he still did.

Moses ends up making the water sweet and they drink.[78] But, soon after this they are all upset and complaining again. They somehow believe they were better off back in Egypt, in bondage, because now they are hungry.[79] What is going on here? The Israelites keep turning their backs on God. They don't seem to appreciate his wisdom or provision.

We often do the same things too don't we? How much do we ignore God's presence in our lives or simply write things off as coincidence? How often do we not trust God is going to take care of our needs? How often do we take God for granted?

This reminds me of a time when my daughter was around three years old. Her mom and grandpa had just been seated at a restaurant. They moved my daughter's plate while they put her in her seat and she started screaming for all to hear, "They're going to starve me! They're going to starve me!" Her mom promptly took her outside, let her calm down, and then explained she would be eating, but her behavior was unacceptable. Then they went inside to eat as they had planned all along. Keep in mind, my daughter was only three, she was a child. But even at three, she could have trusted mom enough to know she would be fed. She had no reason to believe otherwise.

God also heard the grumbling of his children, the Israelites. He heard

---

[76] Exodus 7:14-12:40
[77] Exodus 13:18-14:28 Interesting note here, Often. we simply just want to go back into the fire rather than journey out of it. The people start grumbling and having second thoughts as soon as they see Pharaoh and his army. Okay, I give it to them, I would freak out too. It's early in the game. But, they did actually want to go back. (14:11-12).
[78] Exodus 15:22-25
[79] Exodus 16:2-3

their complaining and provided them with meat (quail) at night and bread (manna) in the mornings. God also provided some conditions concerning the manna so they would not become greedy and take too much.[80] They were to gather only what they needed for each day, discard any leftovers and not to keep it overnight. Still, some did not listen and so ended up with maggots and spoiled manna in the morning.[81] I guess in his own way, God had to take them outside and remind them he would provide for their needs.

God *will* provide what we need, and he wants us to rely on him to provide it. Some of the Israelites had obviously not learned that lesson yet. My daughter learned to trust that her mother would provide. You too can trust God will provide for you. I encourage you to enjoy the journey, even when it's tough. Lean on him instead of worrying or panicking when you don't know which way things will go. With Jesus as your guide, you will be shown many wonders along the way.

Don't Turn Back

Now is not the time to turn back to our old ways. The temptation is there and it may rear it's ugly head seeking to convince us that we will never make it to our promised land. In the beginning of our journey God may seem like a consuming fire, his ways may seem foreign to us, but that is because the toughest part of the journey in many respects, is to focus on the next steps. God gets us started on the path and we simply need to focus on him as he leads the way.

When Moses went up on Mount Sanai and received the ten commandments, the people could see a lot of commotion. Scripture says, "To the Israelites the glory of the Lord looked like a consuming fire on top of the mountain."[82] Moses was there for forty days. During this time the people turned back to their old ways, making idols and worshipping them, no longer trusting in God. [83]

The rest of the Exodus journey continues on pretty much the same. The Israelites continue to complain and grumble. They continue not to trust, then to trust, and then not trust again. It just goes on and on.

I think the answer for our own journeys lie in a couple things. One is

---

80 Exodus 16:11-16
81 Exodus 16:20
82 Exodus 24:17
83 Exodus 32:1-4

learning to discern God's voice in our lives and hearts, and the other is learning how to recognize his miracles.[84]

Let's learn from the Israelites and their journey so our journey can be one with more joy. Let's ask the deeper question: Why did it take God's children over forty years to make this two-to-four-month journey out of bondage to the promised land?

God led the Israelites through the wilderness for over forty years in order to prevent them from going back to their bondage in Egypt. Nearly all of the generation that started the journey out of Egypt never reached the promised land. The simple reason being, they kept turning away from God.[85]

I have seen this play out so often in some of the lives God crosses my path with, especially when coming out of a bad situation. They certainly want help. They are willing to listen to Scripture (or most anything else for that matter) as "self-help," but they are unwilling, stiff-necked, and stubborn when it comes to building a relationship with Jesus. So often, people just can't surrender to their creator in fear of losing control of their lives, when this is exactly what they need to gain the control they are desperately searching for.

Enjoying the Journey

The path of trust and reliance on Jesus is also a journey of joy. Ask God to help you enjoy the journey. It's so easy to overlook and think we'll enjoy things after we arrive. You are on your way to a better place, that is something to enjoy now.

James, Jesus' brother, had some great advice for the road:

> Consider it pure joy, my brothers and sisters, whenever you face trials of many kinds, because you know that the testing of your faith produces perseverance. Let perseverance finish its work so that you may be mature and complete, not lacking anything. If any of you lacks wisdom, you should ask God, who gives generously to all without finding fault, and it will be given to you. But when you ask, you must believe and not doubt, because the one who doubts is like a wave of the sea, blown and tossed by the wind. (James 1:2-6)

---

[84] See Appendix 5: "A Note Concerning Miracles" & Appendix 6: "Hearing God's Voice"
[85] Numbers 32:11-13

FOCUSING ON THE JOURNEY

Notice James adds another blessed statement similar to the Beatitudes: "Blessed is the one who perseveres under trial because, having stood the test, that person will receive the crown of life that the Lord has promised to those who love him."[86]

James has further advice:

> Do not merely listen to the word, and so deceive yourselves. Do what it says. Anyone who listens to the word but does not do what it says is like someone who looks at his face in a mirror and, after looking at himself, goes away and immediately forgets what he looks like. But whoever looks intently into the perfect law that gives freedom, and continues in it—not forgetting what they have heard, but doing it—they will be blessed in what they do. (James 1:22-25)

As I embarked on a new journey out of addiction in the early eighties, I was bound and determined to live life under God's sovereign grace rather than my own self-determination. I still faced many trials, temptations, and a tough road ahead. This journey had started with me accepting God's will to go back into the Army, sign up to be stationed in Germany, and to leave all that was familiar to me. I was given three months to prepare and endure before I flew overseas.

Having recently come clean of drugs, it was still hard to stay that way. By the grace of God, I did stay clean, however, I was still drinking. I was not an alcoholic, but drinking (at least in my mind), helped me to control the urges to use other substances. I can say that I did not get drunk very often, but I want to note two things. First, I am not advocating this as a good method. I am only telling you what happened in my life. Second, drinking almost became the total undoing of all that God had rebuilt in my life up to this point.

It is important for me to share the condition of my heart and circumstances during this period of time because when you are starting a journey out of addiction, the first few months to a year are often the hardest and most grueling. My daily existence was not easy, but my heart was full of joy. I was clearly on the road to a freedom I had not seen in many years. I had been set free and I knew it.

Also during this time, I started going out to a dance club with a girl who

---

86 James 1:12

was as cute as a button. This young woman, Kelly, would become my wife. I would have a beer and she would have a Coke-a-Cola and we would simply sit there for hours talking about life, our lives, and our hopes for the future (not so much our future at this point, but the future).

I was determined to do two things right. One was not to start a romantic relationship. I did not want to find myself on the other side of the world, meet a German girl, fall in love, and possibly hurt this girl back in Florida that I had deep respect for. I had hurt enough people in my life up to this point, and I didn't want to add any more to the list. Second, I was not about to repeat the sins of my past by trying to get her in bed. In my mind, I had ruined the greatest romantic relationship in my life, my first love, by allowing my weakness to take over my goodness. I was not about to make the same mistake, and I am proud to say I did not.

I was embarking on a different way of life at this point and knew it. Yet I was still weak and easily tempted to return to the party life. I was so much in need of mercy and grace, as well as the wisdom and strength of Jesus. The day before I was to ship out to Germany, I went out to the same club alone. I drank, and I drank, and I drank. I did not set out to get drunk, but, I did, very much so. Then, I drove home. This was a terrible decision! I was seeing triple with one eye closed and knew I was in no shape to drive. Then I got pulled over. If I received a DUI, it would immediately stop my enlistment (which, in many ways, was my earthly salvation out of addiction). I can remember being asked for my license, being asked if I had been drinking, and thanking the officer for pulling me over because I knew I should not have been driving.

He asked where I was going. I remember telling him I was going home because tomorrow I would be shipping off to Germany as a soldier. While I deserved to be locked up for a DUI, I was offered grace that day. The officer told me he would follow me home. The last thing I remember was looking over my shoulder as I stumbled in the door to my parents' house and seeing him leave my driveway.

I tell you this because what we do today affects our tomorrow. We can never *expect* grace or mercy, from God, or from the police. But if offered, we must receive it with reverence and repentance. Since that day, I have never driven under the influence, nor will I ever do so again.

> **GUIDING PRINCIPLE:**
> *What We Do Today Affects Our Tomorrow*
>
> Yes, this sounds simple and certainly is understandable, but even more than that—it's profound. We must never go into any situation expecting grace or mercy. We must always seek to do the right thing. We must ealize that EVERYTHING we do today will have an effect on tomorrow.

Shortly after I arrived in Germany I remember waking in my barracks bed and slapping myself on the forehead. What had I done? God had placed a wonderful woman in my life and I didn't see it. I had resisted poisoning the relationship, and more than that, I cared more about her than I cared about myself. This was all so new to me I hadn't realized the treasure I had been given. So I started praying.

God blessed me with this kind and gentle woman and I wanted to bless her. I didn't want to bless her with *me* necessarily, but with someone who would be kind, loving, and godly. I simply prayed and hoped it would be me. We started writing to each other, and the next year, I returned to the United States for our wedding. Two children and five grandchildren later, this year we are celebrating thirty-four years married. My wife is still the same cute-as-a-button-girl I knew back then.

Our journeys are complex. We are not in control. We must wrestle every day to allow Jesus to be more as we become less.[87] Life is about our heart and our motives, and our actions are the fruit of those things. This sounds familiar, doesn't it? We are saved by grace, through our faith, and not by works.[88] Works are the fruit of the mercy and grace is what we have received from God.[89]

As we persevere and seek God's heart, we will find joy in strange places. We will find joy in the face of hardships, struggle, and the fear of the unknown. As we seek God's heart, we will also find treasures that a price tag cannot be put on: blessings, grace, mercy, and forgiveness. The breadth of these treasures are something that can only come from God.[90]

---

87 John 3:30
88 Ephesians 2:8-10; Galatians 3:2 (ESV)
89 James 2:14
90 Exodus 34:6-7; Psalm 86:15

Focusing on the Destination

Your destination may be freedom from a bondage or abuse; it may be the culmination of a calling in your life, or it may simply be to live life more abundantly. The true destination in each of these cases is to live a life in Christ.

Jesus tells us that the kingdom of heaven is right here in our midst and it extends into eternity.[91] I did not start truly living until I died to the world and started living in this kingdom. When I was making decisions on my own they were often the wrong decisions and led me deeper into a bad place. I had to die to the decisions that were based on worldly wisdom, trust God, and start applying his wisdom to my life. When I did, I found that I started living the life I always wanted.

Ultimately there is one destination in life. That destination is the kingdom of heaven. In this kingdom we find the deepness of a relationship with our creator; the gentle yet stern and steady guidance of our teacher and counselor—Jesus. As this kingdom takes root in our own lives we find relationships that have meaning, understanding, and endurance through the tougher times. We have protection from the evil one. We have meaning in our existence, and peace in our souls.

As Jesus explains to us what life in this kingdom is like, he tells us that "the last will be first and the first will be last."[92] What does this mean? Simply put, when our life is only focused on ourselves (and our fallen human condition certainly draws us that direction), we often end up being last. Yet, when we are living for God, and those around us, we often find ourselves being first (yet we weren't trying to be). Simple, right? Let me try to explain.

I have not mentioned this before because in many ways it is immaterial. This period of my life simply blended in with my addicted journey. But, I mention it now because the contrast in these two relationships shares a deep spiritual lesson. I am a used husband (my wife likes to say jokingly), meaning that I was married once before God brought Kelly into my life. In my first marriage, it was all about me. I sought to be first. I was young, met a girl at a beer party, and hit it off. We started living and sleeping together that night and life seemed grand. I soon realized if we got married, we would have more money (you got extra money from the Army if you were married), a bigger place to live, more stuff; I would have someone to cook my meals, to sleep

---

91 Luke 17:20-21
92 Matthew 20:16

with and well, you get the picture, it was all about me. Guess what, it didn't work. I ended up last. Our relationship didn't survive, and we soon divorced.

I certainly didn't want to ever repeat this fiasco. But I really didn't understand any other way to be. We are raised as the center of life with all our needs being taken care of. We are fed, clothed, housed, and often loved, encouraged, and tended to daily. This is good for children as they grow up. But when it remains into adulthood, needing to be the center of the world causes difficulties. Life is to be shared with others. People do not exist simply to serve our needs.

Unfortunately, this is perpetuated by the world throughout life, and yes, sometimes even from our pulpits. Life is all about us. As I said in the introduction of this book, when everything is centered on you, you are more likely to keep coming back for more in that elusive quest to reach the top of the mountain, the ultimate in pleasure, the answer to all questions: *It's all about me, right?* Wrong. When we have this attitude, we ultimately end up last and alone.

When I married Kelly, I was now trying God's ways and recognizing how my ways weren't working out so well. I had a new attitude. I married Kelly to love her, and I cared about how she felt about herself. Guess what, that attitude was reciprocated. I was trying to be last in our relationship but ended up being first, though that was not my intention. The same thing is true in our relationship with Jesus. When we seek his heart wholly and share in his sufferings, we receive his heart in full measure; we receive his healing comfort, his compassion, and his love.[93]

Kingdom living starts with our hearts, not our minds. Our minds can be cognizant of this heart felt attitude, but ultimately it is in our heart where the kingdom will take root in our life. I find that it was a constant battle in my life but as living in this kingdom started to take hold in my heart, it became more and more a natural state of being. Let me say though, our humanness will always creep in so we must be on guard. But, as we look to Jesus each and every day, we will grow, learn, and overcome.

As I illustrated above, this attitude of the heart plays out in our relationships and marriages. It plays out in everything that we do, including our vocations. When we recognize that we ultimately work for God rather than the boss (having godly attitudes and principles), something often changes. We are often less adversarial and more a part of a team. Our focus is more on serving the company and those around us and less on the company

---

93 2 Corinthians 1:3-7

serving us.

In kingdom living, we find strength to face the onslaught of life's trials in ways we never could before. We see those around us with different eyes—with God's eyes. Something grows inside us that we know is not us, it is Jesus' own heart.

Finding the Blessings

Are you generally optimistic or pessimistic? Is your glass half full or half empty? If your answer is pessimistic and you feel you are that way because "life has made me that way" consider trying things God's way.

Look for the good in people, not the worst. Ask him constantly, "Ok Lord, what do you want me to learn from this?" God can take any bad situation and turn it for the good if we allow him.

Remember the DUI that almost cost me my future? God took that and taught me a great lesson. To this day, I will not get behind the wheel after drinking more than one beer. In fact, I even own a pocket breathalyzer to be safe. I rarely use it because I am very stringent on my one beer policy, but I have to say, I do like a good German or Belgian beer. Moderation is the key though, and I believe this is what God intended for us, to live life to the fullest—safely. God can take any situation in your past and turn it to the good if you walk with him and allow Jesus to lead. I am proof!

I have read of killers in prison who find Jesus. They often are instrumental in helping others on their journeys, pointing them to Jesus, the ultimate companion. They may still pay the worldly price for their sin but have found joy as a result of their repentance.

My mother used to tell me that whenever she was feeling down, depressed, or hurting inside, she found great comfort in helping someone. All my life my mother was giving of herself to others in need. She offered an endless supply of encouragement, love, and support to people around her. She taught me what the Reverend Matt Clark vocalized in a sermon he once preached at our church, the simple, yet comforting message: "*Be* the blessing."

Jesus had much to say about serving others. His whole life was built around service. God knows that as we serve others, we are in turn served spiritually in ways we could not imagine. We are not trying to be served, we are simply aiming to serve. This, my friend, is the wonderful upside-down wisdom of Jesus.

Forgive, love, and understand; show compassion, empathy, mercy, and grace. The last will be first, and the first will be last. Remember this wisdom.

Maintaining Your Strength and Health

Journeys are often grueling. That's just how life is. When I was on that month-long sabbatical in the mountains of Tennessee, I spent a lot of my time hiking scenic mountain trails that wound around treacherous rock outcroppings, down along gurgling streams, and sometimes up onto shear rock bluffs thousands of feet above sea level. I learned so many things about hiking and my own journey with God during that time.

First, I never went unprepared. I always had my walking stick, some food, water, a map, and I wore the proper attire. I also took the time to intentionally plan rest stops on these hikes and in my heart. My only companion was Jesus. They were wonderful hikes. I saw his glory way up in those mountains as well as in the valleys below. Every step I took I felt his comforting presence, and when the path got rocky and treacherous, his strength carried me through. Let's take a closer look at some things we can do to maintain our strength and health.

Have the Proper Attitude

I believe that the attitudes we take with us are much like the walking stick I took with me on my hikes. It steadied my way through difficult sections. It also cleared the way as I walked through the thick and sometimes thorny underbrush. Our attitudes steady us as we journey each day. They clear a path, so we don't just barge through the underbrush of daily living.

Seek Spiritual Nourishment

The food and the map I took on my hikes through the wilderness were much like the spiritual nourishment we get from God's Word. We need nourishment along the way to give us strength to take the next step, to go around the next bend in the path. God's Word is our map so we don't get lost. Just like that map, God's Word helps us to reach our final destination.

On my hikes through the forest, I talked with Jesus the whole way. You might be asking, "What do you mean by that Pastor Jan?" I am glad you asked! Prayer and communication is an important component of any journey. Prayer is not always on your knees but is a conversation deep inside with our Lord and Savior. On my hikes I proclaimed his glory every time I looked at the deep green moss-covered forest floor, every time I saw a cascading stream flowing down over a rocky bed, every time I got a view of miles of God's creation in one simple gaze from a mountaintop. I proclaimed his glory when I huffed and puffed up the rocky trails and reached the top of every mountain I climbed.

Wear the Armor of God

The attire I wore for my hikes through the forest was much like the armor of God. I was prepared for the onslaught of nature, rain, and cold. I was prepared for protection from the elements and from the pain I would have otherwise suffered wading through the dense and thorny underbrush in the forest as I journeyed off the beaten path.

Hydrate Your Soul with Jesus as Your Companion

I believe the water I carried was indeed, much like Jesus. We need water to exist, it quenches our thirst. Jesus said he is Living Water. Living water is water that is not stagnant and poisoned. Jesus told the Samaritan woman, "Everyone who drinks this water will be thirsty again [speaking of the water from the well], but whoever drinks the water I give them will never thirst. Indeed, the water I give them will become in them a spring of water welling up to eternal life."[94] Jesus also shared with us, "Let anyone who is thirsty come to me and drink. Whoever believes in me, as Scripture has said, rivers of living water will flow from within them."[95] On many of my hikes I came across rivers and streams of water, fresh and flowing, keeping my body hydrated, just as Jesus keeps my soul.

Take Time to Rest

God's wisdom tells us to take time to rest. Like a T-shirt of mine says, "Jesus took naps. Be like Jesus!"[96] This time of rest is more than just to catch our breath when we get winded, but also so we can take the time to focus on the beauty and blessings around us. This is what rest is for. God commanded a weekly day of rest, called Sabbath.[97] My hikes through the forest demanded

---

94 John 4:13-14
95 John 7:37-38
96 www.memesforjesus.com. Mark 4:38
97 Exodus 16:25-30

stops along the way to rejuvenate my spirit, my body, and my soul.

Life is often exhausting. The journeys which crisscross our daily existence can be frustrating, challenging, and often full of risk. With the right preparation and tools, our journeys can be rewarding, encouraging, and filled with balance. This allows us to see the artistry that surrounds us and the beauty of our destination—the promised land!

8
The Promised Land

"God made it clear in the beginning
that our journey was a journey in relationship with Him.
Through that relationship,
we would become children of the promise."

"The LORD your God will give you rest by giving you this land."

— Joshua 1:13

Wow, we are almost there. This has been quite a journey. I'm tired! I bet you are too! We have spent much of this time together learning to adjust our attitudes, which is a journey in itself. We have learned to find joy in the struggles and to cling close to our guide—Jesus. We have also learned how to navigate the paths we are on. Now that we have discovered and applied these lessons, we must stay strong and disciplined so we can complete the journey.

Getting to this point in the journey, where we can start to see the promised land is wonderful. The natural reaction is to let out a sigh and want to rest. But this leg of our journey may be as hard as when we were starting because our natural inclination is to let our guard down when we can see the prize. But now is not the time to chill.

No matter what kind of journey we are on, whether an altruistic journey, leaving the status quo, or out of a bad place, the changes ahead may seem immense. This is an important moment to remember we have been in the desert, and, until we reach our promised land, we are still in the desert. In many ways we are in a storm of temptations, possible setbacks, decisions, and emotions. Hang on to the truth that there is calm after the storm. We always have something to look forward to.

> **GUIDING PRINCIPLE:** *There is Calm After the Storm*
>
> We often hear there is calm *before* the storm, a period of peace before a crisis. But the truth is, there is often calm *after* the storm. David shared this great truth in one of his songs, "He stilled the storm to a whisper; the waves of the sea were hushed. They were glad when it grew calm, and he guided them to their desired haven" (Psalm 107:29-30).

I remember a long trip my wife and I took to Colorado Springs from Alabama. It was just the two of us, we were going there to rent a house so we could move our family in the coming months. It was a long journey and I was not feeling well. My wife drove as we navigated toll roads, mountains, blocked roads, and a long stretch of barren interstate in Kansas. We were on the road over twenty hours. I will never forget driving through Limon, Colorado on State Route 24 as we descended into Colorado Springs. It was dark when Colorado Springs came into view. We could see the city lights even though it was still in the distance. After our long journey, our promised land was in sight. Our trek had been difficult with me not feeling well. All I can remember is how I so wanted to get there, check into our hotel, and climb into bed. I could see the city ahead of us, yet we still had to travel through the rest of this leg to finish our journey.

We Are Almost There

Now is not the time to set up camp. Now is not the time to speed up, nor is it the time to slow down. The promised land is just ahead. This leg is almost complete. We don't want to lose sight of our goal. If we get too complacent, this last leg of our journey might seem too hard to make. We can't listen to the enemy telling us we can't make it when it is just within reach. The calm after the storm is something we should look forward to, but we never want to prematurely let our guard down. We are not out of the storm just yet.

During their exodus, the Israelites sent out spies to see what was ahead of them. They wanted to know what to expect. In the book of Numbers, Moses tells the spies to be optimistic and to look for the good of the land. He tells them to bring back some of the fruit, so they do. They also report that the land is flowing with "milk and honey," but warn that this last leg of the journey is going to be tough.[98]

One thing I remember about my journey out of addiction is the desire to see the journey end right around the corner. But the truth is, journeys take time. There is so much ground to cover, so much to learn, and so much to see and discover that will help us both now, and on other journeys later in life.

During my time in the Army I was in the Gulf War. My unit arrived in the Saudi Arabian desert when there were still few units on the ground. We set up a defensive perimeter to secure an area for a few thousand soldiers who would arrive soon from our higher unit, the Seventh Corps.

Much like the journeys we experience and even the journey of the Israelites, when we arrived, we had no idea how long we would be in the desert. Every day was a new adventure. We were rarely in one spot long, maybe a few days or a week or two at most. We were almost always on the move. Every day we planned the next operation that would help us accomplish our mission. Some days it was maintenance, some days it was

98 Numbers 13:20-29

THE PROMISED LAND

planning and strategy, other times it was maintaining security for our safety. Some days were full of hardship and struggle, in others we were just plodding on to the next day. But every day there was something new to take in, and every day we were closer to the end of the journey. We were in a war and ultimately our lives depended on our daily survival skills. I learned from every circumstance and every hardship. Finally, six to seven months later, we departed the desert and went back to Germany. After our experience in the desert, Germany was our promised land.

Journeying is never easy. It takes effort and patience. We rarely know when it will end. We must let Jesus lead us every step of the way. We must learn from every situation and apply it as we move forward. We must be strong and courageous and not stay in one place too long when we know it is not our destination. Like the Israelites, our minds can be taken off the journey at hand and we can start to grumble and lose focus. While it is important to take a sabbath rest, it is also important to keep moving after we gain strength and focus from our rest. The Israelites did not do this. Instead they camped, and camped, and camped. As read in the book of Numbers, we see that the Israelites camped out forty-two times from the time they left Egypt to the time they were ready to enter the promised Land.[99] That is an average of a little over a year per encampment. We must always be moving closer to the goal. If we stay on track with Jesus, we will arrive. We will reach our promised land.

The following words should be on our hearts as we journey. They come from Joshua, the commander of God's army after the death of Moses: "Have I not commanded you? Be strong and courageous. Do not be afraid; do not be discouraged, for the Lord your God will be with you wherever you go."[100]

It has been a long journey, you are tired, and the enemy knows you are tired. Pace yourself and get a little rest when you can. You need it for this final leg. Now is the time to just keep on walking. Promised land, here we come!

Continue Walking Don't Run!

If you have been coming out of a bad place, you probably faced a very tough decision to even start the journey. You had to change your way of thinking in many ways and gain the courage to set out toward the promised land. Along the way you probably faced temptations to go back to your

---

99 Numbers 33
100 Joshua 1:9

addiction, abuser, or bad place. The Israelites grumbled to Moses as they came close to the promised land, "If only we had died in Egypt! Or in this wilderness!" they said.[101] Does that sound familiar? You might be saying, "This journey has been tough! Maybe I should just go back. I'm tired. I can't make it."

Maybe you are coming out of your status quo. It also took courage to start this journey. You are making new friends and doing new things. You are stepping out in ways you never have before. Yet something inside wants you to retreat, back inside the shell of life you were leading.

Are you on the altruistic journey? It has been tough, hasn't it? So much to learn. It may seem like there is so much to lose if things don't work out. Looking back at how things used to be seems so much safer than continuing to move ahead.

No matter what, any kind of journey can wear you down. It takes a lot of energy and a lot of time to move from one place to another one. There will always be those temptations just to retreat, to go back to how things were. But don't give up! The promised land is in sight. Jesus is guiding us every final step of the way. Just keep walking.

> ### GUIDING PRINCIPLE: *Just Keep Walking*
> Very often I talk with people overwhelmed by different things in their lives. Sometimes it seems they want to dwell in their overwhelmed state. My advice is: Don't dwell there. Determine the right thing to do and start doing it. Be courageous and start walking out of the place you are in. And then, keep walking. The apostle Paul used this thought of walking quite often. In Ephesians 5:2 (ESV) he tells us to "walk in the way of love" and in 5:8 to "walk as children of light." In 5:15-16, he also warns us to, "look carefully then how you walk, not as unwise but as wise, making the best use of the time." JUST KEEP WALKING.

Your journey has been messy, hasn't it? You have overcome obstacles, temptations, pain, and grumbling. There were times (or there are times) you didn't know what to say or do, which fork in the road to take, how to face your fears, or how to overcome them. Maybe you even felt a little bit crazy to even begin. As you have journeyed with Jesus as your guide, I hope you have

---

101 Numbers 14:2

also found this path to be empowering. I pray you have found a passion you haven't felt in a long time or maybe one you have never felt before.

When I was in the Army I was often attached to infantry units though I was a chemical soldier. The infantry, even the mechanized infantry, walks everywhere. We often walked twenty-five miles with a sixty-pound rucksack and our weapon. We prepared for the journey by carrying a compass, extra socks and first aid for blisters, petroleum jelly for chaffing, and water, water, and more water for hydration. We also carried healthy snacks for energy. We needed a healthy mind to face the pain and messiness of the journey.

We would often start out each day almost at a running pace, but as the day wore on and as we wore out, we would slow down, set a good pace, and stick to it. There is wisdom in that. If you want to make it to the end, you set a good pace.

Remember the Beatitudes? Just like on my Army road marches, we need good attitudes to guide our lives. The Beatitudes are a compass to keep us moving in the right direction. We need God's Word and wisdom as first aid for our blisters and pain, to help us know "how" to journey, as well as healthy nourishment for our mind and soul. Jesus is our hydration. He provides the living water that sustains us.

> Therefore, as you received Christ Jesus the Lord, *so walk in him*, rooted and built up in him and established in the faith, just as you were taught, abounding in thanksgiving. (Colossians 2:6-7 ESV, emphasis added)

Continue walking. Pace yourself. You've come this far, just keep it up and push away the messiness. You're nearly there. You can do it!

You've Arrived!

Congratulations! You have made it to the end of your journey. (For some of you, reading this book was a journey, whew! Well done.) You have now reached your destination—the promised land. If you are on a journey out of a bad place in your life, from addiction for example, the promised land is when you can truly say your addiction has been put behind you. If you are on a journey out of your status quo and your life has new meaning, then you have reached the promised land of that journey. If you are on an altruistic journey into a good place that you have been called, such as becoming a firefighter, then you have reached the promised land of that journey when you realize your dream and are on the crew.

Now that you have arrived, it is a good time to settle in and reflect on all the lessons you have learned on this journey. Now is the time to look back and rejoice in the strength you were given to endure the hardships and temptations in the desert. Make yourself a good cup of coffee or tea and write (or think) some reflections that will help you hold this moment dear in your heart. Most of all, thank Jesus for being your guide. The cool thing is, he wants to continue with you every day. Strong friendships don't fade. Take a breath, smile, and share your journey with someone starting on theirs. You have much joy to share.

Settling in and Not Going Back

Living in the promised land is a great privilege in many ways. There is a community of fellow travelers that, while not perfect, encourage us and walk alongside us. Jesus lives among us and is always there to love, encourage, teach, and guide us.

The real key to living well in this kingdom, the promised land, is lovingly serving each other.[102] We are warned by the apostle Paul that our freedom is not an opportunity to live in the world of fleshly me centered desires, where we would consume each other, but to serve each other in love through showing the wisdom, grace, and mercy of Jesus to others in our lives.[103]

Keep a strong faith, keep your attitudes in check, love God and love each other. Be a good citizen of the promised land. The best news is that you can live here forever, your address will never change.

Now that you have reached your promised land, realize that in some way, after a time, maybe a short time or maybe a long one, a new journey will start. When this happens, pack your bags, get ready to travel, and always enlist your guide; he wants to be with you. As you become a seasoned traveler, journeys turn into adventures, adventures turn into good memories, and good memories feed our souls.

Remember the movie *Karate Kid* from back in the 80's? There is a scene where Mr. Miyagi is teaching Daniel karate under the guise of various chores without him realizing it—wax on-wax off, paint the fence, sand the floor, paint the house, and more.

102 Galatians 5:13-14
103 Galatians 5:15

Journeys are important, just as the various chores were important for Daniel in the *Karate Kid*. The simple chores helped Daniel to see an attitude in karate that he was not understanding. Daniel originally thought it was disciplining his body, but what he learned from Mr. Miyagi was that karate is truly about the spirit.

If we look at the Beatitudes in a similar fashion to how Daniel was learning to view each task he was given, a deep and meaningful transformation takes place. Each attitude is an opportunity to contemplate and apply them to our lives, and, as we come closer to each beatitude, we learn to strengthen these parts of our spirit.

As each individual journey and attitude strengthens our spirit, as we follow Christ, we live in a different place than many of those around us. Daniel found strength in his spirit through learning from his master, Mr. Miyagi. We can find strength in our spirits through learning from our master—Jesus.

> **GUIDING PRINCIPLE:** *Live as a Child of the Promise*
>
> There are few guarantees in this life. Yet, there is one guarantee we do have. As we follow Jesus, we have a freedom in life and a freedom in our travels, that allows us to live in the promised land. It was Jesus who set us free. The apostle Paul tells us in Galatians 4:28 to live as "children of promise."

The real truth about arriving is that we never fully arrive. Another journey begins, and we are always on different legs of this great adventure called life. We are not guaranteed blessing, success, safe passage, or a place in the promised land simply by our birth or because we were born into a Christian family.

But as we follow Jesus, we are set free from bondage and we can enjoy living in the promised land. We are inhabitants of the kingdom of heaven. Jesus said it best: "If you hold to my teaching, you are really my disciples. Then you will know the truth, and the truth will set you free."[104] This was the plan from the beginning. God made it clear that our journey is a journey in relationship with him. Through him, we are children of the promise.

Welcome to the promised land.

---

104 John 8:31-32

APPENDIX

And we know that in all things God works for the good of those who love him, who have been called according to his purpose.

— Romans 8:28

APPENDIX 1

APPLYING THE BEATITUDES

The Beatitudes can be applied to any situation in life. When we apply them, they guide us towards the right course of action. The power in each of these attitudes lies in the reversal of all worldly and human values.[105]

Often people see blessedness as a simple happy feeling, but when Jesus says, "blessed are" and then follows it up with a definition of a blessing for each attitude, this adds up to much more than simple happiness. He tells us that the application of each attitude will result in a good state of living.

Let's look at how we apply the Beatitudes, to honesty:

1. Blessed are the poor in spirit: When we trust in God and don't feel the need to have to lie to gain something in our lives (money, pride, honor, power, or whatever it is we lie to gain) we will find a joy in doing what is right in God's eyes. Situations turn out better in life when I am honest rather than when I lie to seemingly get what I want.
2. Blessed are those who mourn: When we see the wrong of our own untruths and how they hurt those around us, as well as the wrong of untruths told by others and how it hurts those around them, we will find comfort and forgiveness in our repentance.
3. Blessed are the meek: When we are strong in Christ and don't feel the need to lie to increase our status or something in our life, when we accept who we are and accept our wrongdoing by relying on God, we will delight in the resulting abundance of peace due to our honesty.
4. Blessed are those who hunger and thirst for righteousness: When we hunger to be truthful, honest, and to stand behind our word, we will recognize and realize our good position before God.
5. Blessed are the merciful: When we help friends and family around us to see the great truths of God's words, and we live an example of

---

105 Friedrich Hauck and Georg Bertram, "Μακάριος, Μακαρίζω, Μακαρισμός," ed. Gerhard Kittel, Geoffrey W. Bromiley, and Gerhard Friedrich, Theological Dictionary of the New Testament (Grand Rapids, MI: Eerdmans, 1964–), 368.

honesty, it will remind them to extend the same honesty to ourselves and others.
6. Blessed are the pure in heart: When we have discovered these truths and have put honesty to the test, living our lives in God's will, we will see the face of the living God through our eyes of faith.
7. Blessed are the peacemakers: When we, despite the untruths of others, seek not to hate, but to show Christ's love, we will be called children of God because we reflect his character.
8. Blessed are those who are persecuted because of righteousness: When we stand strong in who we are, in truth and in spirit, and don't allow those who make fun of us for being honest or truthful to dull our spirit or to lead us down the wrong path, our reward is the kingdom of heaven where God will more than make up for any suffering or persecution we have endured.

Let's now apply these attitudes to struggles and trouble in our life:

1. Blessed are the poor in spirit: When we trust in God as we face struggles in our life and look to Him for guidance, we share in the reality and promise of the kingdom of heaven.
2. Blessed are those who mourn: When we reflect on who we are and recognize that many times, our struggles are a result of our own doing, we mourn this in our lives bringing true repentance and leading to better decisions next time. When we recognize that sometimes our struggles are the result of someone else's actions, mourn what is happening in their life, and pray for them, we may also see a change in their heart.
3. Blessed are the meek: When we are humble enough to accept our own shortcomings, look to God to help us grow, and strengthen through the struggles or troubles we face, we will delight in the peace and forgiveness we receive from God.
4. Blessed are those who hunger and thirst for righteousness: When we hunger to be truthful, to be honest, and to stand behind our word even in the face of struggle and trouble, we will be filled with goodness from our desire to seek the right course of action in God's eyes.
5. Blessed are the merciful: When we help those in our lives who are faced with struggle and trouble it is indeed a blessing. We pray they will see the great truths of God's words and wisdom. When we are

merciful we are promised that we will receive (and already have) mercy from God.
6. Blessed are the pure in heart: When we have discovered these truths, have put them to the test, and live our lives in God's will, we will be able to see the face of God through our eyes of faith.
7. Blessed are the peacemakers: When we are strong in Christ and don't feel the need to seek retribution or revenge, when we seek peaceful solutions to our troubles and struggles, we will find confidence in knowing we are exhibiting God's character and will share in the glories of the kingdom of heaven.
8. Blessed are those who are persecuted because of righteousness: When we stand strong in who we are in truth and in spirit, we will receive the great rewards of the kingdom of heaven, which will more than make up for our suffering, troubles, and persecution.

As you are faced with different situations in life, look at them through the lens of these attitudes Jesus shares with us. You will find it easier to discover the right course of action in any situation you face and you will experience a better state of living life. At first, applying these attitudes may seem clunky and laborious, but in time they will become a natural way of thinking.

APPENDIX 2

PRAYING WITHOUT CEASING

When I first read we are to "pray without ceasing" in Scripture, I thought, *No way! How can I pray constantly? Sounds great, but it's just not practical.* In time I came to understand the beauty and the depth of the Apostle Paul's words.[106] Let's explore this concept a little more.

There are many different types of prayer:

Prayer at the dinner table
Prayer at the alter in church
Prayer before meetings
Prayer in the morning
Prayer in the evening before going to sleep
Prayer in a group
Prayer when in need
Prayer for someone else's needs

These are all intentional times of prayer, and there are many more. These are all good times to pray.

We know that prayer is communication or conversation, verbally or mentally, with God. Prayer is simply dialogue between you and God— in any form. Prayer is not offered to impress others or a way of manipulating God into giving us what we want.[107]

So, what does it mean then to pray without ceasing? When we are in deep relationship with Jesus, we are in constant communication with him. Yes, we have intentional times of praying. But there is also a litany of small wisps of prayers that constantly go back and forth. In fact, one just left my thoughts this very moment, "Lord, I hope I am explaining this 'praying unceasingly' thing well."

Not all prayer is offered on our knees. Many prayers are offered in the moment, especially when we are in closer relationship with Jesus. Can you imagine going on a journey with someone and never talking to them? Or,

---

106 1 Thessalonians 5:17 (ESV)
107 Matthew 6:5; Mark 14:36

if you had to stop, kneel, and fold your hands together in prayer anytime you wanted to talk, had a question, or asked Jesus for guidance? That would be hard and not too cool. Jesus wants to have a conversation with you, no matter what you are currently doing.

When we are in relationship with Jesus, we should view our whole life, every part of it—the good and the bad—as prayer offered to God. It is a never-ending conversation between us and him.

APPENDIX 3

RECOGNIZING THE OPPOSING FORCES

In simple terms we call this spiritual warfare. This is the struggle we have with the otherworldly forces around us. The Apostle Paul spelled this out in his letter to the Ephesians:

> Finally, be strong in the Lord and in his mighty power. Put on the full armor of God, so that you can take your stand against the devil's schemes. For our struggle is not against flesh and blood, but against the rulers, against the authorities, against the powers of this dark world and against the spiritual forces of evil in the heavenly realms.
>
> Therefore put on the full armor of God, so that when the day of evil comes, you may be able to stand your ground, and after you have done everything, to stand. Stand firm then, with the belt of truth buckled around your waist, with the breastplate of righteousness in place, and with your feet fitted with the readiness that comes from the gospel of peace.
>
> In addition to all this, take up the shield of faith, with which you can extinguish all the flaming arrows of the evil one. Take the helmet of salvation and the sword of the Spirit, which is the word of God.
>
> And pray in the Spirit on all occasions with all kinds of prayers and requests. With this in mind, be alert and always keep on praying for all the Lord's people. (6:10-18)

There are basically three types of spiritual warfare: the world, our fleshly desires, and Satan and his minions. I believe that all three have one common source, Satan. He is the great deceiver, the tempter, our adversary.[108]

Satan doesn't want you to succeed. As a pastor, this has been something I see often and especially after I baptize someone. This very thing also

---

[108] Adapted from Thomas Nelson Publishers, Nelson's Quick Reference Topical Bible Index (Nelson's Quick reference; Nashville, TN: Thomas Nelson Publishers, 1996), 641.

happened to Jesus after he was baptized by John the Baptist.[109]

When we make the important decision to follow Jesus, there are forces that don't want that decision to be made. I often tell people as they prepare to be baptized, that afterwards they might find strong temptations to rescind their decision. This is not always the case, however, I have found this happens often enough.

I remember a girl who was baptized in our church and two weeks later she came to me saying everything was going wrong in her life: she lost her job, the car broke down, and she split with her boyfriend. I counseled her to stand strong in her faith and all this would subside because not even these powers can prevail against us when we have a relationship with Jesus. Today, she is happily married to the young man she split with, and they have a beautiful little girl. She stood strong and withstood the temptations of Satan. Jesus never left her side.

The devil often tempts us when we are most vulnerable—when we are under physical or emotional stress, when we are tired, lonely, faced with uncertainty or big decisions. But we also can find ourselves tempted when things are running along smoothly in our lives, when we feel strong. It is these times when we are most susceptible to pride. We must always be on guard.

The First Type of Spiritual Warfare Is Simply the World.

> What causes fights and quarrels among you? Don't they come from your desires that battle within you? You desire but do not have, so you kill. You covet but you cannot get what you want, so you quarrel and fight. You do not have because you do not ask God. When you ask, you do not receive, because you ask with wrong motives, that you may spend what you get on your pleasures. (James 4:1-3)

The world's wisdom will seek to keep us from succeeding. It says we deserve all kinds of good things. We desire an easy road and an easy journey. When the journey gets bumpy, we often hear that opposing voice inside screaming, "Turn back! You don't deserve this!" I see it all the time, as we

---

109 Mark 1:9-13

journey, the great deceiver will give us a taste of normalcy in our lives hoping to entice us back into the same old routine.

In many ways, especially when on an altruistic journey or journey out of the status quo, worldly things like money, possessions, position, and prestige can keep us back. These things often give us a false sense of fulfillment. Oh, how Satan uses these things to tempt us! And we feel like we deserve those things. Worldly wisdom tells us we do. Sometimes our life is better without all that stuff. Money and possessions are tools in our lives, but when they become the promised land, rather than just tools, we have problems.

I took a pretty sizable pay cut from the corporate world to become a pastor. I was miserable in that world and am much happier where I am now. I am now doing what I feel called to do in my life. And, our needs are still met.

Please remember, especially in the journey out of bondage, but in every kind of journey too, we were already struggling. This struggle was part of what started us out in the first place. Struggle is going to be a part of our lives no matter what. The difference is in choosing to struggle with God at our side. With him, there is always hope. He will carry our burdens.

The Second Type of Spiritual Warfare Is Simply the Flesh.

> Therefore, since Christ suffered in his body, arm yourselves also with the same attitude, because whoever suffers in the body is done with sin. As a result, they do not live the rest of their earthly lives for evil human desires, but rather for the will of God. For you have spent enough time in the past doing what pagans choose to do—living in debauchery, lust, drunkenness, orgies, carousing and detestable idolatry. They are surprised that you do not join them in their reckless, wild living, and they heap abuse on you. (1 Peter 4:1-4)

Ah, the enemy called fleshly desire! What is the flesh? It is our sinful earthly nature.[110] Satan will use lust, sexual immorality, evil desires, and greed to name a few, to keep us from embarking on our journey as well as along

110 Colossians 3:5

the way.

I mentioned the desire for money (greed) above as a worldly weapon used to stop us. Money itself isn't bad but greed is. In the same way, sex itself isn't bad but immoral sex is.

Satan will try to use our earthly desires for sex and money to entice us off God's path and on to the path to destruction. You see, even when we are journeying with God, we are still human and remain lacking in some areas. If you are on a journey towards sexual morality, you will still have the desire for sex and Satan will capitalize on that. Resist the temptation to either stop the journey or to engage in immoral sex to satisfy your desires. The time will come when you have reached the promised land and can possibly enjoy this gift from God in a moral way.

Just remember that the struggle gets better. It took a while for Satan to put you in that bad place and it will take a while for Jesus to bring you back. (He wants you to come back strong and he doesn't want you to ever return to your bondage!)

On those journeys to a better place, it is important not let our guard down thinking things are getting so good that it would be okay to embrace a little affair or a side trip to get rich. Satan wants you to think that. These are journey stoppers! Jesus wants you to keep building up that strength and keep moving forward.

The Third Type of Spiritual Warfare Is Satan Himself.

> Be alert and of sober mind. Your enemy the devil prowls around like a roaring lion looking for someone to devour. Resist him, standing firm in the faith. (1 Peter 5:8-9)

Yep, Satan and his minions are always on the prowl. They will suggest thoughts to your mind, they will place temptations before you, they will suggest a false security, and on and on and on. Beware! It always looks good at first, but once you are enticed in...BAM...they get you, and now you are either back at square one or you give up. Satan's desire is to stop you, slow you down, or take you down the wrong path so you get lost. Don't fall for the deceptions and temptations of the enemy. Be strong, use your spiritual armor—the armor of God—to withstand these attacks.

Take that Satan! I told my readers all about your deceptions. Bye-bye!

APPENDIX 4

THE ARMOR OF GOD: TOOLS YOU NEED ON YOUR JOURNEY

Tools are devices that help us accomplish a task and have specific functions. God has given us tools to help us on our journeys in life. The following tools will help in this war against our adversary, Satan.[111] Take them on your journey, keep them with you, and be mindful of them at all times.

God has provided you with spiritual armor to wear in the battle.[112] These are the virtues necessary to battle Satan and his minions. As you have applied the Beatitudes in your life, you will see that you are equipping your defense against the great deceiver. Wear this armor, use it and defend yourself in this spiritual battle. The apostle Paul tells us, "Therefore put on the full armor of God, so that when the day of evil comes, you may be able to stand your ground, and after you have done everything, to stand."[113]

Belt Buckle of Truth: The reason ancient Roman warriors were able to move freely in battle was because of their belt buckle. They often wore a long flowing robe that would entangle them, so when going into battle they would pull their robe above their knees and use a heavy belt with a buckle to secure it. This enabled them to move about freely without getting tangled. This is also true for you. God's buckle of truth keeps you from becoming entangled in the false truths of this world.

Breastplate of Righteousness: The breastplate is a heavy piece of armor that covers your torso and keeps arrows, knives, and spears from piercing your body, protecting you from mortal blows from the enemy. The same is true with righteousness. Righteousness is doing what is morally and ethically right according to God's wisdom in Scripture. Righteousness protects and strengthens our spirit so we may continue on the journey. When we lie, cheat, steal, have affairs, etc., we leave ourselves open for mortal blows from the enemy.

Your Feet Fitted with the Readiness That Comes from the Gospel of

---

111 Adapted from: R.C. Sproul, *The Purpose of God: Ephesians* (Fearn, Scotland: Christian Focus Publications, 1994).
112 Ephesians 6:10-18
113 Ephesians 6:13.

THE ARMOR OF GOD

Peace: In general, ancient armies moved by foot so protecting the feet was of vital importance.

You will in many senses, also be moving by foot, one step at a time on your journey. If your feet fail you, you will not be able to move forward. The phrase "the gospel of peace" has its roots in the Old Testament book of Isaiah. The prophet Isaiah tells us, "How beautiful on the mountains are the feet of those who bring good news, who proclaim peace, who bring good tidings, who proclaim salvation, who say to Zion, 'Your God reigns!'"[114] The apostle Paul further expounded this thought in his letter to the Romans saying, "And how can anyone preach unless they are sent? As it is written: 'How beautiful are the feet of those who bring good news!'"[115]

Have you ever heard the phrase, "don't kill the messenger"? Very often in ancient days, that is exactly what happened to a messenger who brought bad news, they were put to death.

There is a strength in carrying the good news to God's people. Be a messenger with the good news of the gospel on your feet wherever you go. There is protection in that.

The Shield of Faith: A shield is an important part of a soldier's equipment to help stop arrows, spears, rocks, and such, much like the breastplate. In Roman times, these shields were large. In fact, they were six to eight feet high, rectangular, and designed to basically create a moving wall when soldiers walked forward, side by side into battle. As they approached a city's walls, they would then lift them over their head to stop objects and fire thrown down on them from above.

Look closely at Ephesians 6:16: "Take up the shield of faith, with which you can extinguish all the flaming arrows of the evil one."

Satan doesn't just throw arrows and spears that stab and wound us, he throws flaming arrows which can sear into our flesh and scar us deeply. He can throw accusations and insinuations our way that attack our integrity. Our shield of faith protects us because as we trust in Jesus, we are justified by that faith.[116]

The Helmet of Salvation: The head is a vital and vulnerable part of our body—it contains our mind. The knowledge and hope of our very salvation strengthens us and protects us. Satan wants to wound our mind by creating doubt through lies, that might have us question our hope for eternity with God. Be assured, Satan cannot steal your soul. When we are fixed on our

---

114 Isaiah 52:7
115 Romans 10:15
116 Romans 5:1

relationship with Jesus, we are protected from Satan's deceptions and are given a boldness and confidence in this great cosmic battle. We are told by Paul to put on the helmet of salvation.[117] This knowledge and hope provides protection for our minds.

The Sword of the Spirit: The sword of the Spirit is the only actual weapon mentioned when referring to the armor of God. What is the sword of the Spirit? The sword of the Spirit is the word of God, the Bible.

Jesus is the best example we have in this fight against Satan. Soon after Jesus was baptized, he went into the wilderness, fasted for forty days and forty nights, and was tempted by Satan. Now, I would say, after fasting forty days and nights Satan knew Jesus would be at his weakest. What a great time to tempt him. Satan recognizes when we are at our weakest and that's when he most wants to strike.

The story, from Matthew 4:1-11 goes like this: Jesus was hungry. Satan of course knows this and tells him, "If you are the Son of God, tell these stones to become bread" (v. 3). But Jesus strikes him with the sword of the Spirit: "It is written: 'Man shall not live on bread alone, but on every word that comes from the mouth of God'" (v. 4).[118]

Satan again tempts Jesus by taking him to the highest point of the Holy City and says, "Throw yourself down. For it is written: 'He will command his angels concerning you, and they will lift you up in their hands, so that you will not strike your foot against a stone'"(v. 5-6).[119] Satan is using Scripture too!

Jesus answers Satan squarely with, "It is also written: 'Do not put the Lord your God to the test'"(v. 7).[120] This is like an action-packed movie!

Then Satan decides to pull out the big guns and tempt Jesus with prestige and power.

Satan took Jesus again to a very high mountain and showed Him all the kingdoms of the world with all their splendor. "All this I will give you," he said, "if you will bow down and worship me"(v. 9).

Jesus, true to form, pulls out bigger guns, (actually a bigger sword, oops, forgot we were in ancient days before guns were invented) and hit him with a double blade, "Away from me, Satan! For it is written: 'Worship the Lord

---

117 1 Thessalonians 5:8
118 Jesus' words are actually a verse from the Old Testament: "Man does not live by bread alone, but man lives by every word that comes from the mouth of the Lord" Deuteronomy 8:3.
119 Psalm 91:11-12
120 Deuteronomy 6:16

your God, and serve him only'"(v. 10).[121]

Defeated, Satan leaves Jesus. I love what it says next, "Then the devil left him, and angels came and attended him"(v. 11).

Here is the point: When we couple these pieces of armor with constant prayer and we rebuff Satan, we send him on his way.[122]

---

121 Jesus is quoting a verse from Deuteronomy 6:13
122 Ephesians 6:18.

APPENDIX 5

A NOTE CONCERNING MIRACLES

Miracles happen in our lives every day, but we don't always recognize them. Sometimes we chalk them up to luck or think, "Oh, what a coincidence!"

I believe this might be some of the explanation why the Israelites simply did not see the miracles God was performing in their lives. Scripture tells us they did recognize the parting of the Red Sea as a miracle, but most of the time they grumbled.[123] God kept providing and they just kept moving on and grumbling. I see this a lot today as well. God provides over and over and we just grumble, move on, and then grumble again the next time we are in need.

But Moses saw God's miracles. Why could he see them when most of the time, the Israelites could not? Something I have noticed throughout the Exodus story is that the Israelites were following religion (rules and rituals), while Moses followed and had a deep personal relationship with God.

Understand that under the old covenant, before Jesus and the new covenant, God chose who he would be in relationship with, which was just a handful of people. Upon the death of Jesus, the veil (a large curtain that separated the inner sanctum, the holy of holies, from the outer sanctum) was torn, top to bottom, in the temple.[124] The tearing of this veil removed the separation between sinful people and God. Now, everyone could be in God's presence and have a relationship with him because the sacrifice of Jesus on the cross made us holy in his eyes. God made himself available to everyone—now we do the choosing.

The Israelites sought the practice of religion over God's presence, and so they were detached from him. But, Moses sought and experienced the presence of God in his life. If you look at Exodus 7:1, the Scriptures say, "Then the Lord said to Moses, 'See, I have made you like God to Pharaoh.'" The difference here is relationship. This is also why I think most people still don't see miracles today, they are detached from the living God. Maybe they understand the ritual of religion, but they don't really know Jesus personally

---

123 Exodus 14:31
124 No one could go into the holy of holies, where God's presence was, except the high priest. Even then he could only enter after special cleansing and only once a year. The veil symbolized the separation between God and sinful people. Matthew 27:50-51

in their lives.

The first step to recognizing miracles in your life is to be in relationship with Jesus. Talk to him, listen for his words back to you. Share your life with him and ask him to be a part of your life.

The second step is to recognize those times when you have asked in prayer and then have received.

In my journey out of the status quo, I knew there was more to Jesus and God than I understood cognitively. Yes, I believed, and I knew that I was going to heaven when I died. But what then? Just live until I die? I kept praying and also asking my pastor, "How can I know Jesus on a personal level? What do I do?"

We met for breakfast every Tuesday and he would tell me to find some time daily for quiet time with God, away from distractions. I suggest the same for you. Find time to spend talking to God; making time to listen to his presence and studying the Bible to better know his heart.

I would come home from work at night (I was a financial administrator at the corporate level during this time in my life) and go in the living room to read the Bible and pray. I kept asking God to help me see him clearly in my life.

Each Tuesday at breakfast, I would tell my pastor I was trying, but it was really hard. There were so many distractions when I got home from work. Yet, I kept praying.

Soon, a group of us, including my pastor, went to a Promise Keepers conference for men in Tampa, Florida. It was an overcast day. I was excited because this was my first ever Promise Keepers conference and interestingly enough, the theme for the conference was, "Storm the Gates." Little did I know, I was about to witness two miracles.

So, there we were, in a huge auditorium with probably ten-thousand men. The master of ceremonies came out with much noise, cheering, and fanfare, and welcomed us to the conference. Talk about exciting. He shared the line-up of esteemed speakers for the next two days. He ended his introduction, amid ten-thousand men cheering, with the words, "And now we're going to storm the gates!"

As soon as the word "storm" came out of his mouth a huge thunderclap shook the auditorium. The whole auditorium fell silent. After a moment, the master of ceremonies choked out the words, "Uh, that wasn't planned." That broke the silence, but I knew right then and there the next two days held something big for me.

As I said, I had been wrestling for a long time with trying to find the right time to spend my quiet time with God so that it was just he and me with no distractions. Well one of the first speakers was Bruce Wilkinson, author of the book, "Prayer of Jabez." He was there to talk to us about (take a guess) quiet time with God.

He was adamant we should spend quiet time with God in prayer and study very first thing in the morning. A light bulb went off in my head. I was an ex-military guy and used to get up every day between 4am and 5am. Yes, this was the answer I had been seeking from God.

I turned to my pastor and said, "Hey, that was the answer to my prayer! I need to spend my quiet time with God first thing in the morning!"

I remember my pastor muttering something like, "Not all people are morning people."

I also remember muttering something back like, "He wasn't talking to everyone else, he was talking to me." From that day forward, I arose at 5am and by 5:30 was deep in prayer and study with Jesus. My life changed.

When we ask God, when we cry out to him concerning our needs and the answer comes, we need to be paying attention so we can recognize it. The good news is, as we are in relationship with God, we will come to know his voice more and more.

I could go on and on, story after story, but we just don't have enough paper. The important thing is to live every day in relationship and conversation with our living God, Jesus, and bask in his presence in all that we do. He will make himself known and we will witness miracles that everyone else seems to miss.

APPENDIX 6

HEARING GOD'S VOICE

In the Exodus story, the people didn't hear God's voice, Moses did. At one point, God wanted the people themselves to hear his voice so they would believe, and indeed, this time they did. [125] However shortly after this, they told Moses, "Speak to us yourself and we will listen. But do not have God speak to us or we will die."[126]

So many people today are the same as the Israelites. They have heard God's voice but would rather hear it through someone else, like a pastor or a teacher. Why? Because hearing God's voice is convicting.

The important pre-requisite to hearing God speak in your life is a daily relationship with him. I like to tell people in this hustle bustle age where we are surrounded by so much stimuli it is most important to learn to discern his voice in the crowd. His voice will be heard most often as an answer to conversations you have been having with him. God wants to engage with us, and us to engage in conversation with him. Deep relationship comes out of engaging conversations.

The easiest way to hear God's voice is to take away all distractions and find time alone with him to talk and listen. Moses did this and so did Jesus, all the time.[127] This practice of solitude is important in our lives. It helps quiet all the distractions that pull our minds and hearts every which way. I recommend trying to find time daily that you can be alone with God (quiet time) and intentionally create longer times of solitude—hours, days, even a week or so at times—to withdraw to a solitary place to spend time with God and bask in his presence. As I write this, I am in a cabin, high on a mountain in Tennessee, the solitude surrounds me like a cloak—as does God's presence and voice.

So, what does God's voice sound like? It's gentle, it's thunderous, it's kind, it's comforting, it's convicting, it's soft, and it's loud. The best way I can describe his voice is to use some examples out of my life. As you read these you may remember times he has spoken to you in similar ways (whether you were listening or not).

125 Exodus 19:9, 19
126 Exodus 20:19 (ESV)
127 Exodus 3:1; Luke 5:16; Matthew 26:36-39

Loud and Clear: The most dramatic time I heard the voice of God was after I felt he was calling me into ministry. I was determined to live and learn from his presence in my life and would pray every day, "Lord, show me what you want me to do and I will do it!"[128]

My 92-year-old friend had asked me to come and play guitar the first week after he entered an assisted living facility. I went and played for him, and afterwards, as I was heading home something came over me that I can hardly describe.

I had this feeling like I should place my hands and arms in front of my face to shield myself from some light (I was driving my truck so I didn't physically do this). I felt like God was telling me to start ministering at assisted living facilities through music and prayer. At this point I can only describe the debate with God that went on inside me:

"Lord, you want me to do what? To start a ministry playing music at assisted living facilities? I have two jobs and a family, where will I find the time?" (At the time I had a corporate day job and we owned and operated a candle manufacturing company.)

"Lord, I don't even play or sing well! I haven't really played in front of anyone other than family. How can I do this? I am not good enough."

Despite my debate, I followed. From that time on and for many years, I played every Monday at an assisted living facility in town. I played new hymns and old hymns, prayed with people, and was simply there to bring them joy. And I have to say, it brought me more joy than I could have imagined.

By listening and obeying, God taught me much about myself and others, selfless living, giving, loving, and most of all, how to see people through his eyes. I would have missed all that if I had not listened.

As a Result of Crying Out: It was 1982 in Port Orange, Florida. I was in my tenth year of an addictive lifestyle revolving around drugs. At this point, I would lay in my bed every night crying out to God—literally, night after night—asking him to take these addictions from me.

Those around me probably didn't realize how painful my life was. I hid it pretty well and the next day would just be another quest to party, looking to get high. But God heard me as I cried out to him asking for some sort of solution—all my own solutions had failed—as I knew I was losing my life.

---

128 The full prayer I prayed over and over, and still pray today was, "Lord, show me what you want me to do and I will do it. Lead me every day along the path that I should go. Cross my path with those who need to hear your Word, but also cross my path with those that have a word from you to me."

He answered me in my cry. I saw a TV news show about the new urinalysis drug program the military had called "One Strike and You're Out". I knew this was God speaking to me, so I listened. I went back in the military for the second time, made a career of it, and have stayed clean to this day!

Through His Spirit: I remember the very first time I got up to preach. I was not yet a pastor, had never spoken in front of a large crowd, and had never written a sermon.

Here I was getting up in front of a couple hundred people preaching a sermon titled, "CSI: Christian Salvation Investigation." I was nervous. Yet, just before I got up to speak, a calm came over my heart. Did everything work out well? It did. When you feel the Holy Spirit take over and calm your heart, that's God talking with you.

Through the Study of His Word: I can't even begin to tell you how often God has spoken to my heart when I have spent time asking him to reveal himself through his Word. It has often been life changing for me. One time, I was reading from the prophet Jeremiah. It is probably one of the most recited verses in the Bible, "'For I know the plans I have for you,' declares the Lord, 'plans to prosper you and not to harm you, plans to give you hope and a future'" (Jeremiah 29:11). Wow! Such a beautiful message from God. Then, as I read the next verse I found treasure: "'Then you will call on me and come and pray to me, and I will listen to you. You will seek me and find me when you seek me with all your heart. I will be found by you,' declares the LORD, 'and will bring you back from captivity'" (v. 12-14).

For someone on a spiritual journey (which is all of us), these words ring so true! We can't half-heartedly seek the heart of God and expect to have a relationship with him any more than we can half-heartedly pursue a relationship with our spouse and expect to be close. When we seek God with all our heart he promises to be found. More than that, he will bring us back from captivity and we will find the freedom which is promised through Jesus Christ.

Let me point out that the prophet Jeremiah (and God) was speaking to his people, the people of Israel. It is easy for me to see how this also can apply to us personally now that the veil is torn and no longer separates us from our Father.[129]

The Still, Small Voice: This voice comes most often when I am in a solitary place, but also in times when only a small voice is needed to communicate his heart with me. I find this voice soft, comforting, and often

---

129 Matthew 27:51; Mark 15:38

prodding me in the simple direction I should go. I hear, "It's okay. Forgive. Offer encouragement."

Many years ago, we had our first worship getaway in Daytona Beach. We stayed at a hotel on the beach known for Christian conferences. One morning, I got up very early and walked out on the beach. As the gentle waves swept in I could hear God's voice speaking deep inside my heart. As I looked up and down the beach I could see for miles and miles. This place was an oasis amid a city that was awake 24/7 with partying, sex, alcohol, drugs, and people who thought little about their relationship with Jesus. I found it calming to realize that in all the chaos of life, God's people were here in this city, reassuring the world of hope and love.

I have a friend who once told me she was at a Christian camp, sitting alone out on a dock over calm waters, but her heart was in turmoil. She said that God called out to her, calming and assuring saying, "Be still, and know that I am God!"[130]

Listen for his voice, encouraging you to go the extra upside-down mile; encouraging you to love, to forgive, to be patient, to be kind, or simply, be still.

---

130 Psalm 46:10

BOOK COVER IMAGERY MEANING

He's dressed in ordinary clothes that are not uptight but casual and daily, which we can all place ourselves into. Immediately we can relate. He is wearing a stocking cap which gives the feel it is wet and cold; a place where he has been for a long time in his unpleasant life. He is standing on a hard surface which, though his safe zone, leads to nowhere. Alone and staring out into the vastness of life, he is only a spectator.

He is looking at a blank canvas of calm water which, though it seems easy to navigate without tall obstacles, he knows it will not hold the weight of his problems without some sort of flotation device or vessel. This mirrors his need for help.

Next, he is faced with the huge mountains opposing him. Even if he does get across this lake in his journey, he knows there are still storms ahead. These mountains and storms are the giants who laugh at him, telling him he will never make it to his promised land. They tell him not to even try. They tell him he is the sum of what he has always been, and that no person, not even God, is interested in helping a loser like him.

Still, he is facing forward, looking at the light coming through the clouds. He recognizes there might still be hope. He's afraid but not willing to give up. He's waiting for a guide, for someone to show him how, for someone to reveal what this journey is going to look like along the way. He is looking for a guide who has already been there but has come back for the ones left behind.

There are rocks just under the surface of the water's edge that are revealing to him the first step might not be as hard nor as deep as he thinks and to just take it. They are asking him to leave his long time, going nowhere, comfort zone and place trust in God. They are compelling him to surrender and use the tools that have been placed before him by God for his specific journey. These tools are found in the great conversations with God through Scripture.

Can you place yourself in these shoes? Are you to journey out of a bad place in life or out of your humdrum status quo? Maybe you are ready to embark on a journey into a great new phase of your life and are being called to step out in faith.

For so many of us, this story is familiar. Let's prepare for the *Exodus of Our Lives*!

Jeff DiMario,
President, LARK Global Ministries

ABOUT THE AUTHOR

Jan Puterbaugh has a passion to see people journey in their life with Jesus as their guide. He paid his dues early trying to forge through trials and tribulations on his own but soon realized two major things were missing in his life (well, maybe three). These were: wisdom and a relationship with his creator. Jesus provided both of these. The third thing missing was a partner in life that could put up with his zeal and passion to help others. Jesus also provided this in his wife of now over 34 years.

Jan is retired from the military, which taught him discipline and organization; has owned businesses, which taught him to wear many hats; and was ordained as a pastor in 2008, which fulfilled his life's calling.

He has been known to frequent places most Christians stay away from like bars and homeless shelters, just to get to know people and share in their lives. His band plays often for an organization that feeds the hungry in Sanford, Florida. One of his passions is seeing people reach their promised land.

Jan loves a good German beer, a good cup of coffee, good conversation full of laughter, as well as jamming with other musicians and making good music.

He owns a small recording studio to help Christian musicians record and produce songs as well as those he writes for his wife and for Jesus. His studio, the JamminStation, is one of his favorite quiet places to write and study scripture.

One of Jan's greatest passions is his family. His two daughters and their families live close and gatherings are a regular occurrence. He especially loves spending countless hours with his five grandsons playing pirate games, rolling on the floor, and setting up the church early every Sunday morning.

Connect with Jan at **pastorjan.me** or **facebook.com/jan.puterbaugh**.

www.ingramcontent.com/pod-product-compliance
Lightning Source LLC
Chambersburg PA
CBHW060455080526
44584CB00015B/1439